Behold the Heavens

BEHOLD the HEAVENS

DISCOVERING GOD through the Night Sky

Fr. James Kurzynski

Foreword by Br. Guy Consolmagno, Director of the Vatican Observatory

Our Sunday Visitor
Huntington, Indiana

Nihil Obstat
Msgr. Michael Heintz, Ph.D.
Censor Librorum

Imprimatur
✠ Kevin C. Rhoades
Bishop of Fort Wayne-South Bend
March 28, 2025

The *Nihil Obstat* and *Imprimatur* are official declarations that a book is free from doctrinal or moral error. It is not implied that those who have granted the *Nihil Obstat* and *Imprimatur* agree with the contents, opinions, or statements expressed.

30 29 28 27 26 25   1 2 3 4 5 6 7 8 9

Our Sunday Visitor Publishing Division
Our Sunday Visitor, Inc.
200 Noll Plaza
Huntington, IN 46750
www.osv.com
1-800-348-2440

ISBN: 978-1-63966-257-9 (Inventory No. T2928)
1. RELIGION—Religion & Science.
2. NATURE—Sky Observation.
3. RELIGION—Christianity—Catholic.

eISBN: 978-1-63966-258-6
LCCN: 2025937247

Cover and interior design: Amanda Falk
Cover art: AdobeStock
Interior art: Unless otherwise noted, interior photos are by the author and by Mike Brown of the Chippewa Valley Astronomical Society, https://mba.cvastro.org/. Used with permission.

PRINTED IN THE UNITED STATES OF AMERICA

To the Jesuits of the Vatican Observatory and the presenters and participants of the Astronomy for Catholics in Ministry and Education Workshops

Contents

Foreword

Throughout this book, Fr. James Kurzynski makes reference to the Vatican Observatory and the ACME program. Since I am the Director of the Observatory (and the guy who organizes the ACME program) I thought it might be worth giving you a little background on each of them.

ACME stands for "Astronomy for Catholics in Ministry and Education." It's a week-long immersion workshop where twenty-five participants, mostly teachers or pastors in Catholic schools and parishes, get to know the world of professional astronomy from the vantage point of the Vatican Observatory.

Soon after I had become the president of the Vatican Observatory Foundation (which raises funds for the work of the Vatican Observatory — check us out at www.vaticanobservatory.org), Fr. Kurzynski wrote to me with the idea for such a workshop. We designed it mostly for people like him: pastors who love the night sky and want to know more about how we study it.

Fr. Kurzynski's letter to me was the first of many times the Holy Spirit has sent me just the right person with just the right idea at just the right time. I don't blame the Holy Spirit for the name ACME, however. That was my own fault. You may recall that "Acme" is the outfit who supplies all the tools the Coyote uses in his hopeless pursuit of the Roadrunner, as illustrated by all those wonderful Looney Tunes cartoons I grew up watching. We hope our workshop in the Arizona desert, land of roadrunners and coyotes, will give our participants the tools they need to understand how astronomy and our Catholic Faith work together … without them blowing up in our faces, of course!

The Vatican Observatory itself, which runs this program, deserves a little bit of explanation as well.

Far too many people still think that faith and science don't work together. The idea does not date back to Galileo, though. Galileo remained a good Catholic even after his unfair trial — indeed his two daughters were both nuns! But it comes out of the naive expectation of the Victorian era and its technologists that electricity and steam engines would somehow solve all our problems and make religion obsolete.

The nineteenth century was also the time when Darwin's theory of evolution was being twisted into "social Darwinism" … and worse. The idea that we could preserve the purity of our national blood by keeping out those nasty immigrants from unwanted nations (like my Italian and Irish ancestors) was tied into the anti-Catholic prejudices of that era when the Church spoke out as one of the few voices opposing the inherent evil of eugenics. According to their logic, if the Church opposed eugenics, it must be anti-science; after all, so the myth went, just look what they did to Galileo! (The idea of somehow breeding "superior" people and sterilizing the "unfit" was a widely held pop-science fad of that era, touted by big names like Alexander Graham Bell and H. G. Wells … and other notable scientists who should have known better. Alas, eugenics reached its logical conclusion in the death camps of Nazi Germany.)

In 1891, Pope Leo XIII established a Vatican Observatory at the Holy See, precisely to show the world that the Church supports good science, even as it raised appropriate cautions about technology used for evil. (Technology and its uses, for good or evil, is not the same thing as science, after all … something that people even today tend to get mixed up.)

Pope Leo XIII specifically chose astronomy as the science that the Vatican would support out of its limited resources, in no small part because a Jesuit astronomer earlier that century, Fr. Angelo Secchi, SJ, had earned international acclaim for his work in astronomical spectroscopy. Secchi was the first astronomer to go beyond measuring stars' and planets' positions and instead measure what they were made of and ask how they evolved — the science we now call astrophysics.

Today, following in Secchi's footsteps, we are a dozen Jesuit astronomers at the Vatican Observatory, doing cutting-edge research in fields from cosmology and the Big Bang to the chemical and physical nature of near-Earth asteroids. We maintain our labs and library in the pope's summer gardens of Castel Gandolfo, outside Rome, while also running a modern research telescope on a mountaintop outside Tucson, Arizona (hence our proximity to the Redemptorist Renewal Center, north of Tucson, where we hold the ACME program).

The Observatory exists to show the world that the Church supports science. But why should the Church support science? How does studying the sky bring us closer to God? Ah … that's where my introduction ends, and Fr. Kurzynski's story begins.

— Br. Guy Consolmagno, SJ
March 17, 2025

Introduction

When was the last time you looked for animals in the clouds? It's something we all do as children. The sky, to the youthful heart, is a place of awe and wonder, a place where our daydreams become reality and the world is our playground. For me, these memories evoke peace and joy, a time when I worried about nothing more than the warmth of the sun on my skin, with peace in my heart and the sound of songbirds on a pleasant summer's day.

Did you ever wonder if heaven was in the clouds? Again, a typical daydream of a healthy child. So powerful was this question in my youth that I developed an adolescent theology of heaven being on the light, puffy clouds on a warm day, while the devil rode upon the storm clouds with lightning and fury. Of course, time, age, and experience showed my childhood wonderment to be misinformed. Still, be it seeing mythical animals in the clouds or contemplating what heaven was like, I miss those innocent days.

A less universal experience is to bring that same wonderment to the night sky. For some, gazing into the night sky might have been nearly impossible if you lived in the city. Others may have been afraid of the night, clinging instead to the comforts of a well-lit home. Thankfully, I didn't suffer from either issue in my youth. My parents live in rural central Wisconsin, which blessed me with beautifully dark nights. I was never afraid of the night — instead, I was often outside, just looking at the stars. My first connection with what we call astronomy wasn't through scientific or theological questions, but beauty, beauty that filled me with wonder.

When you turn the page, you will see a panorama image of my childhood view. To the left is my parents' house in central Wisconsin. We would often sit on the back porch and let the days drift by. To the right is a cluster of trees with one solitary light shining through the branches. That light is the bell tower of St. Maximilian Kolbe Church, my home parish. Connecting my childhood home and parish is the Milky Way, ribboned as it always has been on clear nights over the farm.

One evening I was showing my mother different night sky objects through my tele-

scope. I could tell she was getting ready to go inside so, for the grand finale, I announced, "We'll end by looking at the Milky Way." My mother asked, "Where is it?" I simply replied, "Look up."

My mother was slightly disoriented at first, not quite sure where to look. I pointed out the density of stars that stretched from one end of the sky to the other, and said, "That's the Milky Way." My mother was stunned and responded, "I thought that was just some odd cloud that would set in on clear nights." Much to her amazement, she learned for the first time that she wasn't gazing into a cloud, but her galactic neighborhood, her starry backstreets, a swirling sea of wonder. In that moment, I could tell the childlike wonder of looking for animals in the clouds and the spiritual meaning in the thunder had returned to my mother.

I ask you again, when was the last time you looked for animals in the clouds?

Every introduction strives to provide the reader with an understanding of what a book is and is not. So, what is this book? Is this a book of apologetics on faith and science? No. There are many other texts far more adequate to satisfy those needs. Is this an academic book? Yes and no. This book will not feel and sound like a text you would read in the classroom. If you value the "school" of peripatetic learning — learning through engagement of the natural world — then there might be some academic use to this book. Still, the goal here isn't to satisfy classic academic standards. So … what kind of book is this?

This is a book about beauty, about pilgrimage and encounter, about recapturing the awe and wonder you had as a child, regardless of what age you are now. The gear you will need to equip yourself on this journey is simple: the night sky and an openness to how God may speak to you on this journey of encounter and prayer.

Our roadmap on this journey is drawn from reflections from workshops I have been intimately involved with, offered by the Vatican Observatory in Tucson, Arizona. Since 2015, small groups of pilgrims have made their way to the Redemptorist Renewal Center for a week of encountering professional astronomy with the Jesuits from the Vatican Observatory.

Originally, this was called the Faith and Astronomy Workshop. Over time, there was a need to rebrand the workshop, because many came looking for a workshop on apologetics in faith and science. And though this is important, this wasn't our goal. The workshop is now called Astronomy for Catholics in Ministry and Education, or ACME. Our hope was to better emphasize that the goal of the workshop was to have the Jesuits of the Vatican Observatory immerse the participants in the field of professional astronomy. The participants are encouraged through meals, time together on a fieldtrip, celebration of the Eucharist, and quiet time in the Arizona desert to bring their faith to these experiences.

The fruit of this journey becomes something far greater than an academic education you could gain from a book in the library. Attendees gain a most fundamental understanding in order to answer the question, "What is the bridge between faith and science?" The answer is you: You are the bridge. Science isn't a quasi-deity in a dualistic battle with God. Faith and science are things in which people engage to understand the world around them and the God who loves them.

This book will invite you on a similar journey, as I take my prayerful insights from ACME and present them to you. These may not be the same insights all our participants have on our workshops. After all, what they bring with them to ACME is different from what I bring. Still, it will accurately present what I experienced at ACME, both as a participant and presenter, in the hopes of helping God awaken awe and wonder in you.

To assist you in praying with these reflections, I have placed Scripture passages at the end of each chapter. Some of the passages will invite you to go out on a clear night and pray with these passages under the stars. Other passages can be reflected upon either in the privacy of your own home, before the Blessed Sacrament at a church, or in another place that offers you the quiet and comfort to place yourself in God's presence. This book is not primarily a book about definitions of astronomical objects, but an invitation to experience the night sky through biblical eyes.

If this sounds amicable to you, then let us begin our pilgrimage. Let us approach our world with the wonderment of a child. After all, was it not Jesus himself who proclaimed, "Amen, I say to you, unless you turn and become like children, you will not enter the kingdom of heaven. Whoever humbles himself like this child is the greatest in the kingdom of heaven" (Mt 18:3–4)?

There are many dimensions to understanding this passage. One of them is embracing the Gift of the Holy Spirit which we call "Fear of the Lord," but under the positive terms of being in awe and wonder before God and all that he has made. Let us wonder together and together be drawn closer to God through the beauty of the night sky.

– 1 –

Be Still and Behold God's Dwelling

The famous naturalist John Muir spoke of the redwood forests as nature's cathedrals. These massive trees that seem to touch the sky reminded Muir of the spires of the Gothic cathedrals of Europe. When encountering Muir's writings, I was reminded of the symbolism embedded within classical church architecture. Like Muir's playful imagination of seeing redwoods as cathedral spires, so, too, there is a playful dimension to how a church, our sacred space and spiritual home, is constructed and arranged.

When entering a classical or Gothic-style cathedral, you will quickly be drawn to the pillars standing straight and tall. There are often twelve pillars that offer support for a cathedral's structure. For the Christian, these marble sentinels symbolize the twelve apostles, those followers Jesus called to have a unique ministry and mission among the disciples. Thus, to see the pillars of a cathedral with the eyes of faith is to see not only a support structure for a building, but the people who are the pillars of our faith in Christ.

The next thing your eyes may be drawn to is the sanctuary, adorned in a way that draws your attention to a table-like structure of wood or stone. Some may wonder why we call this structure an altar instead of a table. That is because the altar signifies not only the Last Supper Jesus had with his followers but also an altar of sacrifice, recalling the gift of himself that Jesus offered on the cross.

Around the altar are candles, reminding us of how Christ is the light of the world, the promised Messiah whom Scripture foreshadows as that light waited and longed for by the people in darkness. Therefore, a candle ablaze does not merely offer physical light or create an atmosphere of prayer, but reminds us of our light of hope, Jesus Christ.

Most cathedrals, especially those of the Gothic style, draw your eyes upward to the

Scripture

Psalm 8:4–6

When I see your heavens,
the work of your fingers,
the moon and stars that you set in
place—
What is man that you are mindful of
him,
and a son of man that you care for him?
Yet you have made him little less than
a god,
crowned him with glory and honor.

Psalm 19:2–7

The heavens declare the glory of
God;
the firmament proclaims the works
of his hands.
Day unto day pours forth speech;
night unto night whispers knowledge.
There is no speech, no words;
their voice is not heard;
A report goes forth through all the
earth,
their messages, to the ends of the world.
He has pitched in them a tent for the
sun;
it comes forth like a bridegroom from
his canopy,
and like a hero joyfully runs its course.
From one end of the heavens it comes
forth;
its course runs through to the other;
nothing escapes its heat.

vault or ceiling. It is customary for churches to paint the ceiling with stars, once again connecting the structure of the church with the natural world. They are spaces and places of awe and wonder, reminding us of the stars above us in the vault of the night sky.

With this starry vault in mind, I think that if I had met John Muir, I would have eagerly shared with him that, if his beloved redwoods evoke the spires of great cathedrals, then the stars of the sky make the ceiling.

The experience offered in Tucson, Arizona, by the Vatican Observatory concludes with Mass under the stars. The Redemptorist Renewal Center has a beautiful outdoor chapel with the Catalina Mountains as nature's canvas behind the altar. When the sun goes down, the stars reveal themselves as our ceiling, reminding us of what inspired those who adorn the ceilings of some of the most beautiful sacred spaces with reminders of the natural world's luminaries.

Now, I must be careful to clarify that our starry cathedral also presents some challenges. January in Arizona may be warmer than most places in the United States, but night always greets our group with cold temperatures and annoying winds. Between the candles that constantly get blown out and the soft glow of our red lights that protect our night vision, the closing Mass can be a challenge.

Still, it always happens that after the homily, I take a longer pause than usual simply to let our group wonder in silent prayer under the night sky. Occasionally, we'll hear a sniffle from a tear in someone's eye. Sometimes, we'll get serenaded by coyotes. Whatever greets our silence and wonder, the heart always finds peace, resting in God's natural temple of our common home.

We often ask why God created the Earth. The answer we often rush to is that God created the world for us. Though arguments can be made for such an answer, the primary answer to this question is not about us, but the longings of the Divine.

God wanted a home. God wanted a temple. God filled and continues to fill that home with all created things as expressions of his Trinitarian love. We were created in that love to enjoy a unique relationship with God. That relationship invites us to love God freely, but also helps us to see the world with different eyes — not eyes that see a mere collection of atoms, cells, elements, order, and chaos, but eyes that see with God's vision. Eyes that see all things created in God's image. Eyes that see our neighbor as not simply another species but made uniquely in God's image and likeness. And eyes that can see the world as more than just trees, stars, and sky, but also cathedral spires, pillars, altars, and starry ceilings.

God wants us to see with the eyes of John Muir, with the eyes of the mystic, with the eyes of faith. God wishes us to see. And God wishes to be seen through his creation.

Spiritual Exercise

As we begin our journey together, I invite you to enjoy the night under the ceiling of God's natural temple. If you live in a city, drive out to a place that can help you appreciate the beauty of the night sky on a clear night. If being outside at night can make you feel uneasy, bring a friend along with whom you can share your experience. Gaze in wonder at the stars above. Listen for the sacred silence the night offers. Wait for the peace of God to invade your heart. And allow God to write upon your heart what he wishes to share with you in that space.

— 2 —

Contemplating God's Celestial Icons

The closing Mass under the stars isn't the first time the participants of the Astronomy for Catholics in Ministry and Education workshop (ACME) stargaze during the week. Every night, weather permitting, offers an opportunity for our groups to gather, try to find their favorite night sky objects, and look at them through telescopes and binoculars.

In addition to stargazing, the communal aspects of these nights are always a delight. By the end of the week, there will be moments when I look around during an observation session and see that no one is looking through a telescope, but simply sharing stories, laughs, and questions. Some may presume this would frustrate those of us who offer these workshops, but it doesn't. ACME is not only about the observational sciences but also developing a community that finds safety with one another to share questions of faith and science.

Sometimes we're blessed to have people who are doing real-time astro-imaging. With advancements in photography and image stacking, it's amazing how accessible astrophotography has become! Throughout the night, the participants not only have the opportunity to observe the Orion Nebula through a telescope, looking like a gray fuzzball. They also have the joy of seeing what their naked eyes cannot see — an image of the Orion Nebula that contains its rich pinks and wispy clouds that look far more like impressionistic paintings than astronomical images.

Given my love of art, I can't help but think of these objects as God's canvas of creation, presenting us with beautiful "icons" in the sky. In my early years of priesthood, I was trained to "write" icons. For those who are not familiar with icons, they appear to

be rather simple, almost cartoony images of Jesus, saints, and angels. One of the most famous icons is of Christ the *Pantocrator* or Christ the Almighty. He is depicted with the Book of Life in his left hand and his right hand in a position of blessing. Icons are not only images to be appreciated hung on a wall, but a type of written word in image to pray with.

The symbolism and history of icons introduces us to a deep sea of subtle symbolism and meaning. Whether it be the inversion of the colors of Jesus' and Mary's clothes (red and blue) that communicates a unique connection between the two of them, or the gesture of Jesus' hands blessing us (two fingers extended to reference his human and divine natures, with the thumb and last two fingers joined to symbolize the Trinity) there is a lot more to see in an icon than is first perceived.

This deep symbolic meaning that draws us into prayer is why we speak of icons as being *written* and not painted. The goal of the icon is not originality, but to be as exact as possible in replicating the image that inspired the icon. Part of that attention to detail is to accurately present an image of Christ, but is also a call to imitate Christ in our lives. For the one writing the icon, his or her prayer is constantly, "I must decrease, and he must increase" (see Jn 3:30).

Saint Irenaeus uses analogies throughout his writings of God creating like an artist, architect, and monarch in contrast to the Gnostic belief of his time which held that other created things made the world. Irenaeus uses this language to make clear that, although we bear the image of the Creator, the human person creates, but God is the Creator:

> For, to attribute the substance of created things to the power and will of Him who is God of all, is worthy both of credit and acceptance. It is also agreeable [to reason], and there may be well said regarding such a belief, that "the things which are impossible with men are possible with God" (Lk 18:27). While men, indeed, cannot make anything out of nothing, but only out of matter already existing, yet God is in this point pre-eminently superior to men, that He Himself called into being the substance of His creation, when previously it had no existence. But the assertion that matter was produced from the Enthymesis of an Æon going astray, and that the Æon [referred to] was far separated from her

Scripture

Psalm 148:1-3
Hallelujah!
Praise the LORD from the heavens;
praise him in the heights.
Praise him, all you his angels;
give praise, all you his hosts.
Praise him, sun and moon;
praise him, all shining stars.

> Enthymesis, and that, again, her passion and feeling, apart from herself, became matter — is incredible, infatuated, impossible, and untenable. (*Against Heresies*)

Saint Bonaventure states that everything contains some type of God's image and likeness, but the human person contains his image and likeness in a way unique from the rest of creation:

> All these things are traces in which we can see our God. The species as apprehended is a similitude engendered in the medium and then impressed upon the organ. Through this impression, the species leads to its point of origin, that is, to the object to be known. This clearly suggests that the Eternal Light engenders of Itself a coequal, consubstantial, and coeternal Similitude or Resplendence. It suggests that the image of the invisible God, and the brightness of His glory, and the Image of His substance, exists everywhere, by reason of His original begetting, in the manner of the species which the object engenders throughout the medium. …
>
> For all creatures are essentially a certain image and likeness of the Eternal Wisdom, but those that are raised, according to the Scriptures, by the spirit of prophecy to a spiritual prefiguration, are so in a special way; those creatures in whose likeness God willed to appear in angelical ministry are so in a more special way; and those things which He willed to establish as signs, and which hold not only the nature of a sign in the ordinary sense, but also that of a sacrament, are so in a most special way. (*The Journey of the Mind to God*)

Therefore, the night sky bears the markings of the Creator without becoming the Creator. We can come to understand God by exploring how his creation works, and from that contemplation, we can be drawn into a deeper understanding of God.

When I look at nebulae, I feel like I'm gazing at celestial icons. No, these gas clouds from stars that have exploded are not images of Christ, but their striking form presented to us night after night has been painstakingly captured and edited by astrophotographers who try to achieve a faithful representation of the reality.

My favorite nebulae to image are the Horsehead, Flame, Orion, North American, Cassiopeia's Ghost, Bubble, Heart, Soul, and Fish. Just as a child will look for shapes of animals and ships in the passing clouds of daytime, scientists have often given a drab scientific name to nebulae, but also a secondary, more playful name as well — a reminder that even the hard sciences have a lighter side, and scientists are willing to remember that their childhood wonderment still remains along with their scientific research.

ACME makes me think of icons. However, that isn't what comes to mind for all the participants of ACME, and your experience may also vary. Some enjoy the simple process of looking for their favorite constellations. Others like to point out their "homemade" constellations of shapes they've come up with on their own. Others enjoy using the tele-

scopes to look at planets or star clusters. In short, the personal experience of the nights of observation can vary greatly, but the unifying factor is that we are all gazing upon the same night sky. We are all gazing upon the same fingerprints of the Creator. And we are all trying to understand our place in this creation and our relationship with the Creator.

A few years back, Pope Francis proposed new corporal and spiritual works of mercy: To protect God's creation and to contemplate God's creation. Though these proposed works of mercy have not been widely embraced, in my approach to the night sky, the contemplation of creation makes sense.

If I can contemplate the masterful works of Van Gogh and come to know a bit of this impressionist master, why not come to know God — the Divine Artisan — through his creation? In this contemplation, we do not worship the night sky as God, but we receive a glimpse of the "Master's brush strokes," making us wonder how great is the Glory of God in comparison to the beauty and glory we behold in the stars of night.

Spiritual Exercise

As a follow-up to the last chapter's theme of drinking in the beauty of the night sky and God's love, if you can, go out again to a place where you can behold the heavens. There, quiet your heart and ask, "How does what I behold bear the beauty of God's image?" When you have explored this expression of beauty, take some time to realize that no matter how beautiful the night sky might be, it pales in comparison with the beauty that is you, me, and the Mystical Body of Christ. And it doesn't even approach the transcendent glory of the Father, Son, and Spirit.

— 3 —

Celestial Storytelling

The human person, regardless of culture, embraces storytelling. A good story can inspire, teach, entertain, warn, remind us of the past, foreshadow the future, or help us see things through new perspectives. Stories often utilize sign and symbol to draw the story-receivers into a deeper understanding of themselves and the world they live in.

This mix of story and symbol is at the heart of Jesus' use of parables to teach his followers. These stories are so impactful, we need only hear the subject of each to be reminded of the lessons they contain. I would guess that you could provide me with at least a summary of what Jesus was trying to communicate to his followers if I asked you for the meaning of mustard seeds, yeast, lost coins, lost sheep, weeds, pearls, and scattered seed. And if we are willing to allow our spiritual imagination to play, simply encountering things like seeds and weeds in our everyday life can be transformative in turning our mundane, daily experience into a constant reminder of God's love for us through natural sign and symbol.

This natural storytelling doesn't stop at the weeds in your flowerbed, but expands to the sky. Ancient Mediterranean cultures devised a system of storytelling by grouping stars into constellations. These stories have been so enduring that I would venture to say many of you know some of the basic constellations to this day, whether it be the Big and Little Bears (reimagined as the Big and Little Dippers), Orion the Hunter, Scorpio, or Cassiopeia. The ancients wanted to make a connection with the night sky through story.

Human storytelling may have played some role in the development of Chinese constellations or asterisms. Chinese asterisms are divided into twenty-eight mansions based on the moon phases. Despite their differences, the visual connecting of stars reminds us of an internal desire to have our story "up there" in the night sky and to have what is going on "out there" be meaningful in our daily lives.

In the first gatherings of the Vatican Observatory's workshops, Nancy Lebofsky would offer presentations on Native American constellations, along with simple classroom projects to teach children about these celestial stories. While listening to her stories, a question emerged: Was there a common source or inspiration that each culture drew from when constructing these star stories? As it pertains to Native American culture, the only common connection I have been able to find between these and other cultural understandings of constellations is the night sky itself. What is it about the night sky that is so powerful, so resonant with the core of the human person, that we want our story to be in the night sky and also want the night sky to be meaningful in our daily lives?

The Judeo-Christian approach differs slightly from those of other cultures. Scripture definitely includes stars as a storytelling tool, but in a slightly different manner. For example, when God is establishing the covenant with Abram, changing his name to Abraham, he uses the stars as a metaphor to teach Abraham about the fruitfulness of the divine

Scripture

Amos 5:6–9
Seek the Lord, that you may live,
lest he flare up against the house of Joseph like a fire
that shall consume the house of Israel, with no one to quench it.
The one who made the Pleiades and Orion,
who turns darkness into dawn,
and darkens day into night;
Who summons the waters of the sea,
and pours them out on the surface of the earth;
Who makes destruction fall suddenly upon the stronghold
and brings ruin upon the fortress,
the Lord is his name.

Job 9:7–10
He commands the sun, and it does not rise;
he seals up the stars.
He alone stretches out the heavens
and treads upon the back of the sea.
He made the Bear and Orion,
the Pleiades and the constellations of the south;
He does things great and unsearchable,
things marvelous and innumerable.

promise being established. It doesn't take much imagination for me to try and understand how Abraham must have felt when the words were uttered by God, "Look up at the sky and count the stars, if you can. Just so, he added, will your descendants be" (Gn 15:5).

I like to pray with this passage at a quiet, dark location outside of the city where I live. I will listen to the silence the night provides, interrupted on occasion by the calls of birds nesting for the night, the cries of fox and coyote, and the deep hoots of owls while I just look at the stars as they shimmer. I then talk with God about my day, expressing gratitude for good things, sharing my concern over the bad things, asking forgiveness for sins committed and blessing for family and friends in need.

The phrase "Count the stars, if you can" has become a type of prayerful mantra in these moments. As I share my heart in prayer, the silent, shimmering beauty of the stars not only wraps me in celestial beauty, but is also a reminder of a promise — a promise similar to God's speaking of a rainbow as a sign and symbol that he will not destroy. The stars remind me of God's promise of faithfulness, fruitfulness, and happiness in your life and mine.

If we pray under a starry sky, does that mean we are worshiping the stars? No. In the Book of Job, God corrects the suffering protagonist with the words, "Have you tied cords to the Pleiades, / or loosened the bonds of Orion?" (38:31). I hear in this both a story of God's creative act and omnipotence and also a reminder that God is not one god among many, but the one God who created all things. We are simply gazing at the Divine Master's artwork as we would observe a painted masterpiece in a museum. And in the process, we come to realize that we, too, are also one of God's masterpieces. A broken masterpiece?

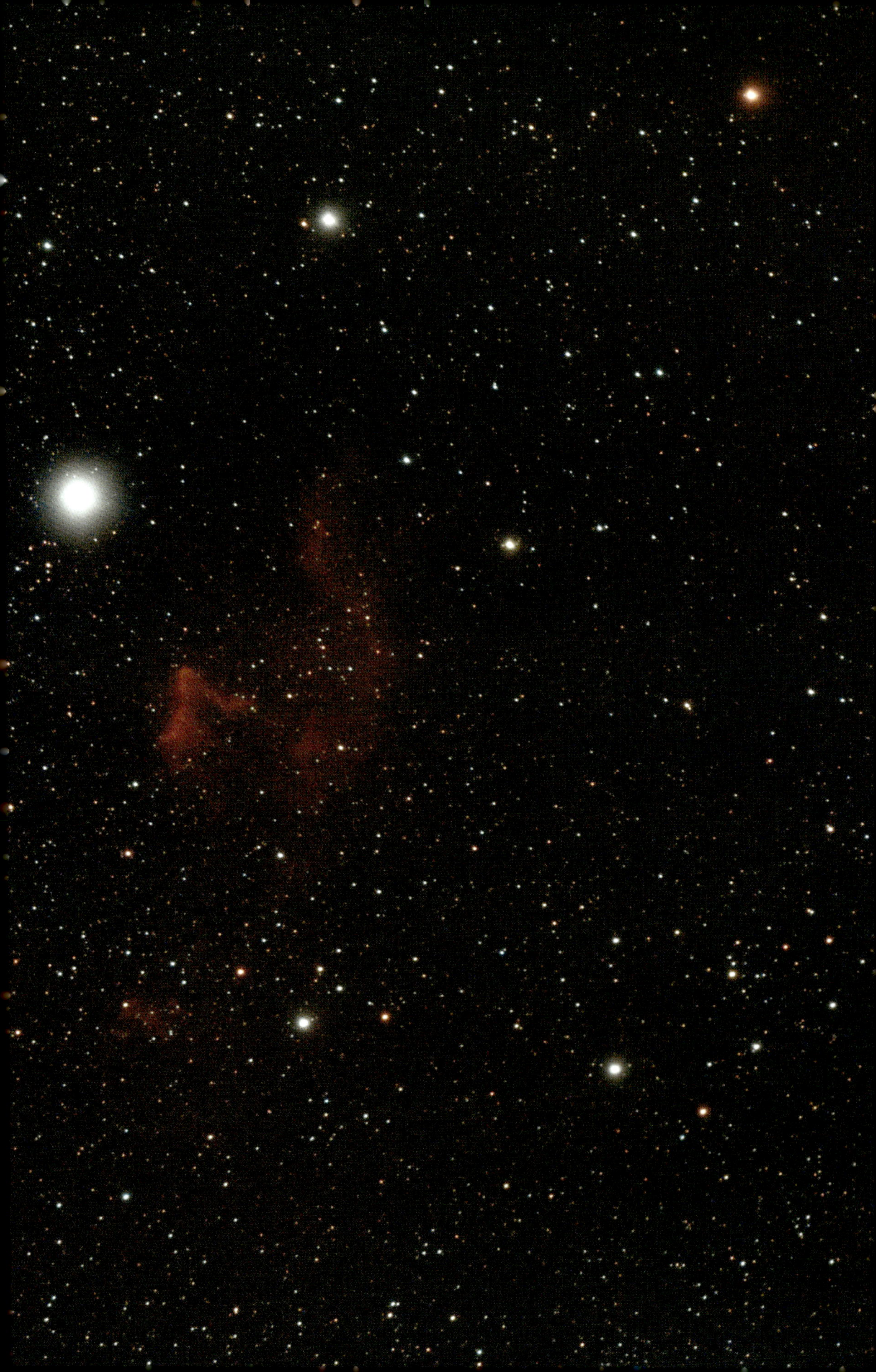

Yes. But a masterpiece that has been curated and restored by the Master Artist's grace.

When considered in this manner, we begin to see that the Judeo-Christian approach to the stars is one of playful sign and symbol. Like the parables, we can use them as a means to help us be taken in awe and wonder of the world around us, but then to transcend that beauty to encounter the God who brought all things into being.

Spiritual Exercise

I would invite you to find your favorite story in the Bible about stars. On a clear night, go to a quiet place with dark skies and listen for the silence of the night. And as you are serenaded by the sounds of creation resting for the evening or awakening from its daylong slumber, count the stars if you can, read the Scripture passage you have chosen, and discover the divine story in that moment which is your story. Allow the playful intuition we all have to imagine our stories in the stars and give yourself a joyful moment of rest. Allow yourself to be still and know that, despite the brokenness we all possess, you are loved by God, your story matters to God, and you are one of God's masterpieces.

— 4 —

Skipping Interstellar Stones

Have you ever wished that you could hold a piece of outer space in your hand? As you may or may not know, it is easier to do this than you think! In the last chapter we explored the storytelling of constellations. This chapter will focus on meteorites and the stories they tell.

At our ACME workshop, Dr. Larry Lebofsky (husband of Nancy) shares his expansive knowledge of meteorites with the group. Dr. Lebofsky is a Senior Education and Communication Specialist at the Planetary Science Institute and an Education Specialist at the University of Arizona. Dr. Lebofsky's presentation is to help us understand the difference between a meteorite and a "meteor-wrong." What's a "meteor-wrong" you may ask? A stone that isn't a meteorite.

Larry gives the participants different types of stones of all kinds of shapes, sizes, and colors and has us work in groups to determine whether what we're looking at is a meteorite or not. We are given simple tools, a magnifying glass and a magnet, to look at smaller details and see if the stone is iron-rich or not. By the end of the exercise, we have been given very basic tools to help us understand the science of how to identify a space rock and how that understanding can help tell a story about where it's from, what it's made of, and what the ancient solar system may have been like.

After our class, we usually do a field trip to see meteorite collections and learn how scientists use their knowledge of meteorites to tell the story of how our home was made.

These presentations and visits always remind me of Saint Bonaventure's classic, *The Mind's Journey to God*. In this work, Bonaventure explains a mystical experience he had that revealed to him how we ascend to truth through the six-winged seraph first seen by St. Francis of Assisi. Bonaventure looks for Trinitarian patterns of coming to know God. Drawing upon biblical images and applying them to our experience of God and the world, he develops a threefold ascent based on a threefold pairing of the seraph's wings:

Scripture

1 Peter 2:6–8
"Behold, I am laying a stone in Zion, a cornerstone, chosen and precious, and whoever believes in it shall not be put to shame." Therefore, its value is for you who have faith, but for those without faith: "The stone which the builders rejected has become the cornerstone," and "A stone that will make people stumble, and a rock that will make them fall." They stumble by disobeying the word, as is their destiny.

Matthew 16:13–19
When Jesus went into the region of Caesarea Philippi he asked his disciples, "Who do people say that the Son of Man is?" They replied, "Some say John the Baptist, others Elijah, still others Jeremiah or one of the prophets."

He said to them, "But who do you say that I am?" Simon Peter said in reply, "You are the Messiah, the Son of the living God." Jesus said to him in reply, "Blessed are you, Simon son of Jonah. For flesh and blood has not revealed this to you, but my heavenly Father.

And so I say to you, you are Peter, and upon this rock I will build my church, and the gates of the netherworld shall not prevail against it. I will give you the keys to the kingdom of heaven. Whatever you bind on earth shall be bound in heaven; and whatever you loose on earth shall be loosed in heaven."

> So this is the three-day journey into the wilderness, or the three degrees of light within a single day: dusk, dawn, and noon. It represents the triple existence of things, that is, existence in physical reality, in the mind, and in the Eternal Art, according to what is written: Let it be; God made it; and it was. It also represents the presence in Christ, our Ladder, of a triple substance, bodily, rational, and divine.
>
> Corresponding to this triple movement, our mind has three principal powers of perception. One is aimed at the material world and is called *animal* or *sensorial*; the other is aimed inward and acts within itself, and is called *spiritual*; the third one is aimed above itself, and is called *supernatural*. By these triple means, we should dispose ourselves for the knowledge of God, and love Him with our whole heart, and with our whole soul, and with our whole mind. In this consists the perfect observance of the Law, as well as full Christian wisdom.

From this introduction onward, we come to understand this process in a way applicable to our modern world. Bonaventure invites us to understand God by encountering and engaging the natural world. To do this, we are to study, classify, and define the natural world around us to help deepen our understanding of what it means to say that all things are made

in God's image. The second step is to distinguish how the human person made in God's image and likeness differs from the rest of creation. Last, Bonaventure invites us to embrace that which transcends the natural world in the ultimate ascent into the arms of God:

> Open your eyes, then, alert your spiritual ears, unseal your lips, and apply your heart, so that in all creatures you may see, hear, praise, love, and serve, glorify and honor your God, lest the whole world rise against you. For the universe shall war … against the foolhardy, whereas it becomes the foundation of glory for the wise, who can say with the prophet: For You make me glad, O Lord, by Your deeds; at the works of Your hands I rejoice. How great are Your works, O Lord! — In wisdom You have wrought them all — the earth is full of Your creatures.

What I love about Bonaventure's approach is that it's a way to understand faith that starts with engaging with the natural world. The first step of his ascent affirms the fundamental goodness in all created things, while also resisting the temptation to reduce creation to the tangible and measurable.

Through the eyes of Saint Bonaventure, science is a necessary aid in this process of ascent through engagement. Whether it be understanding the different kinds of meteorites, stars, planets, dwarf planets, exoplanets, moons, asteroids, or the other wonders found in the night sky, we gain knowledge about the wonder of God's creation, and what seems profoundly distant from us becomes inseparably close.

The humbling realization about Bonaventure's first step of ascent is precisely that it is the first: It's the beginning of our ascent to God. This is why science, from a spiritual perspective, falls nicely into the category of Fear of the Lord. This gift of the Holy Spirit does not mean that we are afraid of God, but instead that with this gift we possess a healthy fear that we might wound the most important relationship of our lives. And when we embrace that relationship, we are humbled in awe and wonder at the glory of God and how that glory is expressed through creation — whether in the shimmer of the stars of night or the jagged edges of the stony meteorite.

Spiritual Exercise

I would encourage you as a spiritual practice to go for a walk in a field or by a shoreline and pick up some stones that you find interesting. Examine each one and ask basic questions about the object you see: What is its color? How dense is the stone? How hard or soft is the rock? Does it look like other materials may be mixed with the stone? And ask other questions that naturally emerge when examining these stones.

Contemplate the wonder of God's image being present in everything around you, even in the handful of stones that you hold. And wonder how, as a creature made in God's image and likeness, you are given the gift of making such distinctions and growing in knowledge through that awareness.

— 5 —

Location Matters

Location matters, in both our spiritual lives and astronomy. Though it is true that a person can pray anywhere, there are times when our surroundings can distract us. Personally, I find that my prayer life flourishes more in quiet, contemplative environments, free from distraction and the sound of other voices.

Regarding communal prayer, my heart gravitates toward environments that are supportive, intentional with their awareness of each other, and committed to living an outward-focused life. I am a fan of more traditional Church architecture, but Solomonic columns and a triumphal arch design are secondary if the communal dimension lacks a genuine sense of Christian charity.

Location and atmosphere are very important in having a meaningful interaction with the night sky. True, stars can be seen in the city and the countryside, but one quickly learns the true impact of light pollution after spending time at a true "dark sky" location on a clear night.

The proper tools can also greatly help to enhance our experience of the night sky. Central to ACME is taking field trips to professional observatories and active space missions to learn about the tools that professionals use to gaze at and travel through the night sky. The locations we've traditionally visited are NASA's OSIRIS-REx Mission Center and the observatories atop Kitt Peak and Mount Lemmon.

On September 8, 2016, NASA successfully launched the OSIRIS-REx mission. This mission didn't have the glitz of glimpsing a distant dwarf planet like Pluto, but it was designed to visit a close neighbor to earth called Bennu. Bennu is an asteroid that is on the list of near-earth objects which pose a threat to our common home. Bennu has a slim chance of hitting the earth in the twenty-second century. However, this isn't the only reason NASA has chosen to visit Bennu.

After a year of building up the probe's speed through a process that used the gravity

Scripture

For your prayer, I would invite you to pray with the story of the Ethiopian eunuch who is struggling to understand a passage from the prophet Isaiah. While it's not directly related to the wonders of the night sky, I encourage you to focus on the desire to find someplace and someone to help bring clarity to your faith journey.

Acts 8:26–40

Then the angel of the Lord spoke to Philip, "Get up and head south on the road that goes down from Jerusalem to Gaza, the desert route." So he got up and set out. Now there was an Ethiopian eunuch, a court official of the Candace, that is, the queen of the Ethiopians, in charge of her entire treasury, who had come to Jerusalem to worship, and was returning home. Seated in his chariot, he was reading the prophet Isaiah.

The Spirit said to Philip, "Go and join up with that chariot." Philip ran up and heard him reading Isaiah the prophet and said, "Do you understand what you are reading?"

He replied, "How can I, unless someone instructs me?" So he invited Philip to get in and sit with him.

This was the scripture passage he was reading:

"Like a sheep he was led to the slaughter, and as a lamb before its shearer is silent, so he opened not his mouth. In (his) humiliation justice was denied him. Who will tell of his posterity? For his life is taken from the earth."

Then the eunuch said to Philip in reply, "I beg you, about whom is the prophet saying this? About himself, or about someone else?" Then Philip opened his mouth and, beginning with this scripture passage, he proclaimed Jesus to him.

As they traveled along the road they came to some water, and the eunuch said, "Look, there is water. What is to prevent my being baptized?" Then he ordered the chariot to stop, and Philip and the eunuch both went down into the water, and he baptized him.

When they came out of the water, the Spirit of the Lord snatched Philip away, and the eunuch saw him no more, but continued on his way rejoicing. Philip came to Azotus, and went about proclaiming the good news to all the towns until he reached Caesarea.

of the sun and planets to "slingshot" it to its destination, OSIRIS-REx arrived at asteroid Bennu in 2018. Before making contact with Bennu, it orbited the asteroid to learn everything it could about its composition and find a safe touch point for the probe. This process took two years to complete before OSIRIS-REx performed its primary mission of touching down on the surface of Bennu, sucking up some of the material of the asteroid, quickly leaving its surface before it got stuck, and returning the sample to Earth.

It was hoped that the "asteroid vacuum" on the bottom of OSIRIS-REx would suck up between 60 grams and 2 kilograms of Bennu's surface. It came back with a bit more than hoped for! Why did NASA see this type of mission as important? With a pristine sample of Bennu that is not contaminated by our atmosphere, scientists hope to learn more about the origins of our planet. Asteroid Bennu is like a solar system time capsule, untouched for billions of years. It is a remnant from when the Earth and other planets were created. The hope is to learn more about our material origins by studying the sample captured by OSIRIS-REx. Research shows that Bennu is carbon-rich, teasing out the possibility that this asteroid contains ancient building blocks for life.

Another amazing trip was going to see the massive Mayall Telescope atop Kitt Peak with its four-meter primary mirror. Its immense size demonstrably shows the scale of tools needed to peer into the deepest recesses of the known universe. When we visited this massive telescope, it was the first time I had seen a telescope I could literally fall into. In some ways, it reminded me of the first time I walked into St. Peter's Basilica and felt dwarfed by its size, beauty, and history. It was truly overwhelming hearing about the Mayall Telescope's discoveries, its ongoing scientific work, and how all the telescopes atop Kitt Peak have contributed to our understanding of the universe.

Future ACME workshops featured trips to Mount Lemmon. On those trips, I took joy in watching our participants have their first experience of seeing large telescopes. Seeing their wonder and awe at these tools of research reminded me of my initial experience on Kitt Peak.

During our ascent to the peak of Mount Lemmon, we first visited the peak of Mount Bigelow with its sixty-one-inch telescope. We moved about the grounds in relative quiet so as not to disturb the sleeping astronomers preparing for their night shift. When this and the other telescopes of Mount Bigelow and Mount Lemmon were first built, they were considered cutting edge, the best of the best. Now, with the advent of larger ground bases and groundbreaking space telescopes, professionals find these scopes less desirable.

Ironically, this insight into the rapid pace of progress in the science of astronomy points out a seeming disconnect between faith and science. Faith places deeper emphasis on unchanging truths that are timeless in nature, while science races to advance the technologies needed to observe what at times seems a timeless universe.

After completing our time on Mount Bigelow, we continued our bus pilgrimage to the summit of Mount Lemmon with its observatories. Mount Lemmon has a rich history, as it was a military communications base for nuclear missiles during the Cold War. The land has transitioned mostly to a place of scientific research, with a small section still operated by the Air Force. Mount Lemmon truly is a powerful story of turning "swords into plowshares" (Is 2:4).

As we visited the various telescopes, we were quickly reminded of how thin the air is at elevations over 9,000 feet. During our lunch, Br. Guy Consolmagno, the current

Director of the Vatican Observatory, told us to observe how the bags of potato chips we brought for lunch had expanded, looking like overinflated balloons. As we walked around the observatory, the light air was causing some embarrassing guttural struggles due to the same forces that caused the expansion of our potato chip bags. We found humor when Br. Guy shared his version of Carl Sagan's line, "We are all stardust." Br. Guy affirmed, "We are all a bag of chips."

During one of our trips to Mount Lemmon, we had the honor of meeting Gregory Leonard, discoverer of Comet Leonard and researcher of near-earth objects. Standing with him and the telescope he used to discover Comet Leonard was inspiring. It was equally fascinating to hear how his primary work is identifying objects that could pose a threat to the Earth. Mount Lemmon presents itself as a powerful paradox for our time: A place once dedicated to the study and development of weapons that could destroy the world now exists as an astronomical watchtower in the hopes of helping to avoid the destruction of our world.

When I asked Dr. Leonard what he personally loves to explore in the sky, he simply said, "I love being able to discover new things every night."

Discover something new every night. What a beautiful sentiment for people of faith to hold on to!

We always encourage our participants not to make ACME the only time they visit places like observatories and mission sites. God has blessed me with the opportunity to visit several space mission centers in addition to our ACME workshops. In 2018, I had the privilege of visiting NASA Goddard Space Flight Center where the Parker Solar Probe was built and prepped. Through a generous invitation by *Sacred Space Astronomy* reader Leonard Garcia, I had a hands-on look at the NASA Goddard campus.

Leonard did a beautiful job explaining the work of NASA Goddard, sharing his joy and energy for the groundbreaking work that is done at this facility. Toward the end of the tour, Leonard walked me past a pressure chamber that was testing the resilience of the Parker Solar Probe. Just before leaving this visit, I decided that I wanted to travel and see the probe's launch. Sadly, that trip never occurred, but being present at Goddard and learning of the mission gave me a deep feeling of connection with the mission.

As I've shared with you already, when you visit sacred places or places dedicated to some of the most amazing astronomical research in the world, the words *awe* and *wonder* are often the most fitting to describe the experience. They are words that, in relation to the Sacrament of Confirmation, communicate the Holy Spirit's gift of Fear of the Lord. They are also terms that can communicate human experiences when we are stopped in our tracks and reduced to amazement at what we behold. Whether it be wonderment at St. Peter's Basilica, the gift given through the Sacrament of Confirmation, or your first experience of a huge telescope, exhilaration in and awe of these intentional spaces is a universal experience.

Spiritual Exercise

What are your sacred places? Where do you go to discover or be discovered by God? Who are the people associated with these places that help you understand the deeper significance of these locations? Where are places that help you feel more deeply connected with the natural world? Do you find that you can come to know a little bit of God by encountering creation? Who are the people who accompany you on this exploration?

Have you ever wanted to know more about the night sky? Have you ever wanted to know more about how to grow in your faith life? Even if your answer is "no," I would encourage you to visit a local observatory on a night when they do public observation. Reach out to a local parish to ask if you could talk with someone about working on deepening your faith life. The local observatory or the local parish may not have the grandeur and awe-inspiring impact of places like Mount Lemmon and Saint Peter's, but they can be powerful places of learning and for connecting with people who are passionate about faith and science. Perhaps in those environments, you may have a deepening of your understanding of God through faith and reason.

Location, location, location — it's all about location. Sacred spaces do matter. Places that explore space matter. Seek these places out, learn about them, learn from them, and allow God to expand your understanding of faith and the world around you.

— 6 —

A Cloud of Witnesses to Inspire Us

Who are the people that inspire you? Who are the people you desire to imitate, at least in part, to become a better person? When I think of this question, I recall a whole list of heroes and inspirations going back to my childhood and continuing through my adult years.

Some of those names have changed while others remain. As many young men do, I dreamt about being a professional athlete, an astronaut, or some other heroic profession. Yes, I always thought of priesthood, but those childhood inklings were more curiosity than discernment. Later in life, when the idea of priesthood remained, those musings transformed into more intentional exploration. I started to look for examples after whom I would want to model my ministry. In addition to my parish priest, Fr. John Swing, I also was inspired by well-known saints like Fr. Maximilian Kolbe and lesser-known holy men like Bl. Solanus Casey and Ven. Samuel Mazzuchelli. I could go on about how each inspired me to be a priest, but the main point is that we all have a desire and need to look to others to understand who we are in God's eyes, and then live in that tension of emulating our heroes while also allowing the uniqueness of who we are to shine forth.

At our ACME conferences, there are always presentations on prominent figures in astronomy who should be known and admired for their contributions. Some of those figures are Catholic clergy and religious, but also laity who pursued an understanding of the natural world in profound ways.

In addition to historic figures of science, the presenters who share their knowledge of these key people stand themselves as inspirational figures. Whether it be Chris Graney and Br. Robert Mache of the Vatican Observatory sharing insights on figures of faith and

> Pope's position was both precarious and ambiguous.
>
> Spain claimed to support Catholicism against the Protestant Germans, but both the Pope and Catholic France were worried about Spain's growing power. Throughout, Galileo's wealthy patrons in Tuscany, the Medici, were keeping a careful neutrality.
>
> Interestingly, the Galileo trial was launched right at the time when the war was at a crisis, so perhaps it was designed as a distraction to keep pressure off the Pope.
>
> In any event, none of the explanations (except the "myth") have science versus religion at the core of the Galileo affair.

In the process of addressing the Galileo affair and learning about significant Catholics of faith and science, what begins to emerge is a truer narrative of Catholicism: The Church has long been the support and patroness of the sciences.

Long before Sr. Mary Kenneth Keller's groundbreaking work in Computer Science, a Catholic laywoman by the name of Laura Bassi (1711–1778) was the first woman to achieve a doctorate in modern science and the second woman to hold a university professorship in Europe. Prospero Lambertini, the Cardinal of Bologna who would eventually become Pope Benedict XIV in 1740, was the patron of Bassi's education. Pope Benedict XIV even named Bassi to an inner circle of scientific minds in the Vatican who were promoting the modern sciences after the sad events of the Galileo affair. Needless to say, the true relationship between faith and science is far more complex and rich than one finds on the surface.

The examples of clergy and religious who were groundbreakers in the sciences reaches a crescendo with a diocesan priest from Belgium by the name of Monsignor Georges Lemaître (1894–1966). It is a common misconception that the Big Bang Theory (the scientific theory that at the time of this writing stands as the best explanation of the origins of the universe) came from Albert Einstein. Though Einstein's Theory of Relativity is at the heart of the Big Bang Theory, the "Father" of the Big Bang Theory is Monsignor Georges Lemaître, a Catholic priest who was also a brilliant scientist.

Monsignor Lemaître did not coin the title "The Big Bang," but he saw in the equations of Einstein a "cosmic egg." Einstein held that the universe was stagnant, with no beginning or end. Lemaître saw in the Theory of Relativity an expanding universe. And if the universe is expanding, it also means that the universe was much smaller at some point … very, very small. Therefore, Lemaître shared his idea of a cosmic egg with the best scientific minds of the time, and his theory was met with hesitation. The idea that the universe had a beginning and is expanding toward an end flew in the face of the accepted science of the day. The idea of the cosmic egg was mockingly dubbed by some in the scientific community as "Lemaître's 'Big Bang Theory.'"

Time, however, vindicated Lemaître, and though the advancement of science continues to tweak and deepen our understanding of the Big Bang, the core science of Lemaître is still accepted. Will there be something that will replace Lemaître's theory in the future? Perhaps, but his contribution will always stand as a true pivotal moment in our search to understand the universe.

These presentations on inspirational figures of science at ACME always stir up two insights for me. First, Catholics shouldn't fear science but should engage it as part of our embracing of faith and reason. Second, we can learn a great deal about humility when learning about role models of faith and science in our lives.

Science is not only open to being wrong, but always has a self-critical eye, presuming that there is always a deeper and better language to be discovered to explain the world around us. This is a difference between theological doctrine and scientific theory: Doctrines of faith are unchanging while being open to language to deepen their understanding, while scientific theory, though intellectually very sturdy with key foundations that don't change, is always open to the proverbial monkey wrench in the machine that might fundamentally alter our understanding of the world around us. Still, the professional humility of science that presumes no theory is complete can inspire people of faith never to presume our faith journey comes to completion here on earth.

As a person of faith, what can you learn from the humbling nature of science? Though we would not jettison core doctrines of our faith, are there ways to deepen our understanding which would dispel misconceptions and errors to help us grow in our knowledge and practice of faith? Have we closed ourselves off from change, making God's work of calling forth in us the person we are to be more difficult? Are we open to being humbled so God can build us up and deepen our understanding of ourselves, our relationship with the world, and our relationship with God?

Spiritual Exercise

It can be difficult to avoid the trap of thinking that being a faithful Christian means we can never admit a lack of understanding of our beliefs. Standing in awe before the night sky (or any aspect of creation) opens us up to the God of transformation so we can become who we were made to be: an expression of God's love in the world. What is an aspect of the created world that you wonder about? Can you take that wondering to prayer?

— 7 —

Harbingers of Doom or God's Glory?

Most of the reflections I am presenting to you in this book are invitations to see beauty, peace, joy, and wonderment in the objects of the night sky. However, there is a far more troubling aspect to these same objects, both spiritually and astronomically. There is an uncomfortable elephant in the pages of this book that must be addressed: the connection between events in the night sky and judgment.

For example, I have been blessed to witness and image two once-in-a-lifetime comets: Comet Neowise and Comet C/2022 E3. Both comets were stunning to see in the night sky and provided moments of joyful contemplation. I recall one night when I was observing comet Neowise on the banks of the Chippewa River just north of Durand, Wisconsin, when the thought occurred to me, "How can people see these beautiful objects as something foreboding and laced with a narrative of doom?"

Regarding comets, the Bible doesn't specifically mention these celestial visitors. Some have associated them with references to "stars falling from the sky" or the "wandering stars" mentioned periodically in apocalyptic passages. If these passages were to be reduced to actual astronomical phenomenon, it would make more sense to see stars falling from the sky as meteors and wandering stars as planets (since their paths across the sky are not synchronized with the rest of the stars).

What makes more sense is to regard astronomical events as symbolic references to a world that is out of sorts. To help us enter into this approach, I will need the help of one of my former teachers, Bishop Robert Barron, and his understanding of rose windows and medieval spirituality.

Bishop Barron, in his book *Heaven in Stone and Glass*, speaks passionately about

his love of the circular stained-glass windows called "rose windows." These windows are called such because they form the shape of flowers with the petals containing images of private and public life. Bishop Barron explains that these windows in medieval spirituality communicated a well-ordered soul, where the entirety of creation was in right relationship with God and with itself.

With a rose window symbolizing a well-ordered world as our backdrop, we can then see that a symbolic representation of sin in the world would be if the petals of the rose were to fall. If the spiritual key to rose windows is to communicate a world in right relationship, then stars falling from the sky and failing to give their light, the sun failing to shine, and eclipses symbolize times when we are not in right relationship with God and each other. To put it more simply, stars "behaving badly" can be a reminder to us of how we behave badly through sin and need to be healed and put back into right relationship with God.

Before we completely move away from the science of astronomical events, we should presume that this negative connotation of comets, meteors, and eclipses most likely came from real-world events. For example, I have yet to read an account of an asteroid hitting the earth as a positive event. These are events that cause great destruction and death. Modern science rightly warns that if a comet were to hit the earth, it wouldn't be a bad idea to make a good confession and pray with the fervor of Advent for Jesus to come

Scripture

The following Scripture passages reference astronomical events. As you pray with them, focus less on the events mentioned, which can cause people to experience fear and anxiety. Focus more on Jesus' call for us to stand confidently with our heads held high, trusting that the only thing we need to fear is separation from God's love.

Luke 21:25–28

There will be signs in the sun, the moon, and the stars,
and on earth nations will be in dismay,
perplexed by the roaring of the sea and the waves.
People will die of fright
in anticipation of what is coming upon the world,
for the powers of the heavens will be shaken.
And then they will see the Son of Man
coming in a cloud with power and great glory.
But when these signs begin to happen,
stand erect and raise your heads
because your redemption is at hand.

Jude 1:11–21

Woe to them! They followed the way of Cain, abandoned themselves to Balaam's error for the sake of gain, and perished in the rebellion of Korah.

These are blemishes on your love feasts, as they carouse fearlessly and look after themselves. They are waterless clouds blown about by winds, fruitless trees in late autumn, twice dead and uprooted.

They are like wild waves of the sea, foaming up their shameless deeds, wandering stars for whom the gloom of darkness has been reserved forever.

Enoch, of the seventh generation from Adam, prophesied also about them when he said, "Behold, the Lord has come with his countless holy ones to execute judgment on all and to convict everyone for all the godless deeds that they committed and for all the harsh words godless sinners have uttered against him."

These people are complainers, disgruntled ones who live by their desires; their mouths utter bombast as they fawn over people to gain advantage.

But you, beloved, remember the words spoken beforehand by the apostles of our Lord Jesus Christ, for they told you, "In [the] last time there will be scoffers who will live according to their own godless desires." These are the ones who cause divisions; they live on the natural plane, devoid of the Spirit.

But you, beloved, build yourselves up in your most holy faith; pray in the holy Spirit. Keep yourselves in the love of God and wait for the mercy of our Lord Jesus Christ that leads to eternal life.

quickly. My point with these examples is not that we should reduce astronomical events solely to a symbolic meaning, but rather that symbolic meaning in Scripture is meant to help evoke a real change of heart in our relationship with God and one another.

In many ways, this chapter communicates the tension we can feel in our hearts when it comes to events in the night sky. We wonder at their beauty with an unsettled awareness of their potential for destruction and violence.

Thankfully, astronomical events in the late twentieth and early twenty-first centuries point to the symbolic understanding of their presence. We have been able to wonder at their beauty and find peace in their occurrences. Still, it is easy to find real-world conflicts in war, pandemics, and global struggles that can give our hearts a moment of pause. This tension reminds us of the tension in Jesus' life, death, and resurrection: Jesus established the kingdom of God through his life, death, and resurrection, but its full awareness is still slowly unfolding in our lives.

This chapter evokes the type of discussion that occurs during our breaks, meals, and road trips at ACME. Over the many workshops we've had, I've been asked about my thoughts on evolution, alien life, the end times, and a whole plethora of other common questions people of faith have.

I've also had discussions of a far more personal nature about children or friends who have fallen away from their faith, claiming that science is the reason for this removal of God from their life. Again, to give voice to the community that ACME forms, the discussions do not only revolve around comets, planets, nebulae, and dark matter. They also explore who we are as people with our hopes, dreams, fears, and joys. Many times, the questions explored don't have easy answers. However, the journey we make together on our pilgrimage of the mind and heart gives comfort that we often share the same dreams and fears.

Spiritual Exercise

It's challenging to encourage a spiritual exercise for you at the end of this chapter because the events I've mentioned are rare by nature. However, what is more accessible is to talk with people we know and trust about the tough events in the world around us that awaken these questions. Whether or not you have seen a lunar eclipse, a solar eclipse, a comet, or a meteor shower, or need to depend upon the experience of others in that regard, reflect on those experiences and reflect upon them with others.

— 8 —

A Liturgical Cosmos

In the previous chapter, we explored the question of whether astronomical events should be seen as something to fear or something to enjoy. As with most things in Catholicism, we arrived at a both/and approach: Sometimes we can see their beauty and sometimes they should give us concern. We can both revel in their beauty and see them in a symbolic way as a call to conversion.

This chapter will stretch the symbolic meaning of these events and encourage us to see them through liturgical eyes. What does that mean? The word *liturgy* in Catholicism usually refers to the celebration of Mass. *Liturgy* is a word that really communicates a well-ordered communal act of worship and prayer. Can we see the night sky as a type of natural "liturgy"? Let's explore the question and see where it takes us!

When a priest or layperson helps prepare for Mass, they refer to a small book called an "*Ordo*." This Latin word literally means "order," and the book lays out the elements of each Mass from the feast days, readings, and special aspects of a given Mass. It presents to us the "boring" aspect of Mass, providing the structure for our communal prayer.

When these simple, ordinary elements of communal prayer are structured and executed with sincerity and openness to God's grace, powerful moments can occur in the heart of the congregation. This is the heart of what the Second Vatican Council called "Noble Simplicity." Noble simplicity is the notion that when we do the small, ordinary actions of liturgy with sincerity, reverence, and simplicity, moments of closeness with God can be achieved. Our theology of the Mass speaks of this act of liturgy as entering into the timeless, where the earthly and heavenly liturgies meet or kiss in an act of love with God. (We'll explore this understanding of God's timelessness in a future chapter.)

We can see this beautiful understanding of simple, ordinary human actions evoking powerful spiritual experiences as analogous to how the movements of the night sky can evoke powerful experiences in our lives.

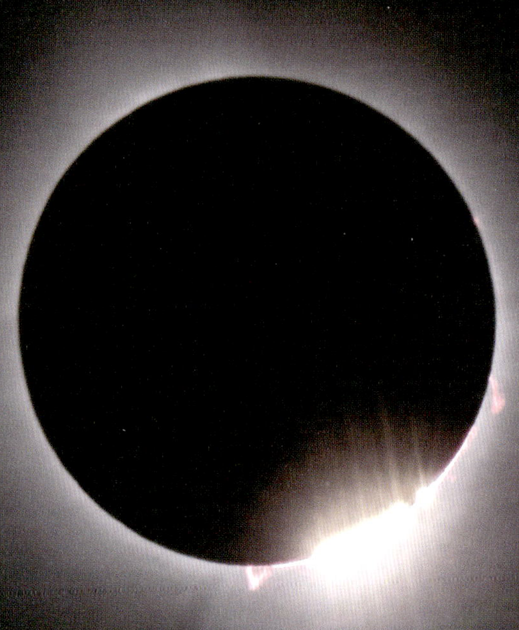

To begin this exploration, can we see an *ordo* in the night sky? Yes! The movement of all celestial objects develops predictable patterns in the night sky. Calendars and seasons are informed by the appearance of constellations and lunar phases. So predictable are these patterns that we can know the position of the stars from thousands of years past and into the future.

Amid these predictable patterns are unique moments when the *ordo* of the night sky can present an event of wonder. One of those events of wonder is a total solar eclipse. As you may know, a total solar eclipse is a rare event when the moon passes between the earth and the sun at the precise distance to block out the sun while revealing the corona of the sun in a spectacular manner. To see the corona with the sun completely covered is called "totality."

Most people don't get the chance to experience totality during a solar eclipse. Totality can only be experienced along a thin corridor. The typical experience of an eclipse is to find creative ways to look at the sun indirectly by creating shadows through leaves or some type of homemade device. If you're lucky, you might know someone who has a telescope with a proper solar filter that allows you to safely look at the sun or know someone with a welder's mask that provides the same protection for your eyes. Seeing an eclipse in this way is still exciting, but nothing beats the experience of seeing a solar eclipse in totality!

When I talked with friends of mine who experienced totality, they spoke of differing but equally powerful experiences.

One of my closest friends in the priesthood is Fr. Brian Konopa. He is also a priest of the Diocese of La Crosse, and we worked closely together when I was the chaplain at Regis High School in Eau Claire, Wisconsin. Fr. Konopa and I are very different people. He's very "Type A" in his approach to priesthood, while I'm a bit more "Type B." He's quite analytical and less emotional about faith, while I tend to have more of a romantic heart in my approach. I mention this because it was an odd irony in 2017 when Fr. Konopa ended up experiencing a solar eclipse in totality, while I did not. Fr. Konopa has little interest in things like eclipses. It's not a bad thing, it's just who he is, but he was visiting some classmates of his in Lincoln, Nebraska, that year and unexpectedly planned his trip at the time of the solar eclipse.

When I asked Fr. Konopa what he thought of the eclipse, I was surprised at his response: He told me that it was a *religious experience*. For Fr. Konopa to say he had a religious experience watching the eclipse spoke loudly to me of the power of the moment.

To Fr. Konopa, the most impactful moment was during the end of totality when the second "diamond ring" appeared. The diamond ring is an event that occurs at the beginning and end of a total solar eclipse when craters on the moon's surface allow light to be seen, which creates a type of diamond-ring shape around the moon.

In vivid detail, Fr. Konopa explained how he felt like he was at the tomb of Jesus when the second diamond ring occurred. At first, he was simply trying to be attentive to the shimmering light of the sun through the moon's valleys, accentuated by the solar

Scripture

Luke 24:13–35

Now that very day two of them were going to a village seven miles from Jerusalem called Emmaus, and they were conversing about all the things that had occurred.

And it happened that while they were conversing and debating, Jesus himself drew near and walked with them, but their eyes were prevented from recognizing him.

He asked them, "What are you discussing as you walk along?" They stopped, looking downcast. One of them, named Cleopas, said to him in reply, "Are you the only visitor to Jerusalem who does not know of the things that have taken place there in these days?"

And he replied to them, "What sort of things?" They said to him, "The things that happened to Jesus the Nazarene, who was a prophet mighty in deed and word before God and all the people, how our chief priests and rulers both handed him over to a sentence of death and crucified him. But we were hoping that he would be the one to redeem Israel; and besides all this, it is now the third day since this took place. Some women from our group, however, have astounded us: they were at the tomb early in the morning and did not find his body; they came back and reported that they had indeed seen a vision of angels who announced that he was alive. Then some of those with us went to the tomb and found things just as the women had described, but him they did not see."

And he said to them, "Oh, how foolish you are! How slow of heart to believe all that the prophets spoke! Was it not necessary that the Messiah should suffer these things and enter into his glory?" Then beginning with Moses and all the prophets, he interpreted to them what referred to him in all the scriptures.

As they approached the village to which they were going, he gave the impression that he was going on farther. But they urged him, "Stay with us, for it is nearly evening and the day is almost over." So he went in to stay with them. And it happened that, while he was with them at table, he took bread, said the blessing, broke it, and gave it to them. With that their eyes were opened and they recognized him, but he vanished from their sight.

Then they said to each other, "Were not our hearts burning [within us] while he spoke to us on the way and opened the scriptures to us?"

So they set out at once and returned to Jerusalem where they found gathered together the eleven and those with them who were saying, "The Lord has truly been raised and has appeared to Simon!" Then the two recounted what had taken place on the way and how he was made known to them in the breaking of the bread.

prominences. Then, it happened. The light of the sun turned a stunning white, allowing the diamond ring to appear. Fr. Konopa said it was an experience so powerful that it made him wonder if this is what the Roman soldiers experienced when the stone was being rolled away from the tomb after the Resurrection. I could tell that the experience had a deep impact on him.

"James, you HAVE to go and see totality sometime in your life!" he told me.

I replied, "Brian, events like this help people understand why I like to 'geek out' about astronomy so much!"

He began to laugh, affirming not only his positive experience with totality but his new insight into me, adding a new dimension to our friendship.

Another friend of mine, a Doctor of Microbiology by the name of Anne Geraghty, also experienced totality and was eager to share her experience over a cup of coffee. Anne's trip was a bit more colorful and comical than my brother priest's. After recounting the troubles she faced actually getting to a place where she could camp out to view totality (ending up on a farm with the guest bathroom in an underground bomb shelter), Anne began to share her experience of the event.

Predictably, Anne's explanation as a scientist was less religious and more attentive to the particulars of the unfolding of totality. Anne is a "birder," having cataloged an impressive life list of bird observations in addition to participating in bird count research with numerous organizations. She shared two articles with me from eBird, a citizens' science program out of Cornell University that asked its participants to track bird behavior during totality. She explained that certain songbirds will start their morning calls shortly after totality is completed and night hawks will begin their evening routine during totality. Though her description was more scientific than spiritual, what came to mind was how this experience impacted more than just its human observers; all of creation participated in this event.

The main theme of Anne's experience was how quickly everything happened, but also how long-lasting the impact has been upon her since the event. When I asked Anne if she had a religious experience during the eclipse, she struggled to find the right words. She explained how her spirituality as a biologist is deeply connected with the outdoors. She has been to most of the major national parks and sought out rare and pristine regions of our planet's environment. Anne explained that of all the experiences she has had on her travels to some of the most beautiful places on Earth, totality was more impactful than all of them. She also affirmed that the spiritual meaning for her was still being unpacked, that she was still trying to digest the brief moments of totality. Similar to my priest friend, Anne said to me, "You *have* to experience totality at some point in your life! You of all people!"

Both of these conversations I mention lasted about an hour and a half, with the majority being a monologue from my friends who wanted to share their experience of totality with me. At their prompting, I was both inspired and blessed to experience totality in 2024. My experience was slightly different than those of my friends in 2017, since I was

also a presenter at the total solar eclipse retreat in Bloomington, Indiana, organized by Fr. Timothy Sauppé.

In my presentations at the retreat, I encouraged the participants not to focus on the "harbinger of doom" approach to the eclipse. Instead, I encouraged them to let God play with them and let their experience be their own.

My encouragement to the retreat participants also raised a question I need to reflect on in my own experience: Did God "play" with me during the eclipse? It's hard to put into words what I experienced in totality. I loved listening to the birds start their evening song as the sun's light dimmed. It was fascinating to see our shadows become well-defined and sharpened as the limited light brought a crispness to what we saw. I enjoyed the sudden cool of the day, since it had been quite warm.

I found the most joy in helping people see the slow progression of the eclipse through my little h-alpha telescope (a telescope designed to safely view the sun). And it was powerful to behold the diamond rings both at the beginning and the end of the eclipse.

Still, I struggle to give a concise description of my experience. Perhaps that's a good sign. Maybe it points to a time of inner play with God. What if God wanted my experience to be a slow burn instead of an instantaneous moment to be quickly moved away from? Or maybe it was an experience of natural liturgy in which God took the simple movements of creation and arranged them in a way that communicated his love for me and filled me with awe and wonder.

As I concluded my conversation with Fr. Konopa about his experience, he simply said, "James, a thought hit me while I was watching totality: When was the last time people really looked to the heavens?" I knew, intuitively, that his statement was both literal and metaphorical. In the literal sense, we discussed how astronomy was once the science of priests who used it to construct calendars and establish feast days. In the metaphorical sense, he also implied that we need to gaze in awe and wonder not only at the beauty of creation, but also upon God who brought all things into existence.

So, how is a total solar eclipse like a "natural liturgy"? Some of my parishioners will levy the complaint that Mass is boring, the same thing every week, and needs a little more life and excitement. At the same time, there are celebrations of the Mass that parishioners identify as powerful and life-changing, renewing their love of God. Sometimes I even hear from people how they felt that time "stood still" during the Mass.

I find the range of emotions and experiences regarding Mass is similar to that of a total solar eclipse. Some may dismiss the idea of making a nine-hour drive or an eleven-hour flight to see a total solar eclipse, seeing it as a waste of time for something that lasts about two minutes. Isn't an eclipse just the simple movement of the Earth and moon around the sun? What's so special about that?

From a very different perspective, by listening to my friends' powerful recounting of totality and recalling my own experience, the answer to the question, "Why would someone drive nine hours to experience something that lasts only a couple of minutes?" becomes clear. The answer is rather simple, but equally life-changing: There are experiences in life worth having, in which two minutes can contain the joy of eternity.

Spiritual Exercise

For this chapter, I invite you to pray with the story of the Road to Emmaus (page 70). Obviously, this isn't a passage about astronomy, but it speaks to how one's heart can come alive when everyday actions are met with God's grace. After reading this passage, ask the question: How does God speak to me through the liturgy? How does God speak to me through simple, daily activities which, when brought together, provide moments of wonder?

— 9 —

A Sacramental Cosmos

One of the central aspects of the Catholic liturgy is providing an encounter with the mystery of God's love. The word *mystery* in modern English can communicate something that is obscure and difficult to understand, or something hidden that needs to be discovered. In the ancient Church, the word *mystery*, derived from the Greek word *mysterion*, was the word Eastern Christians would use to refer to what we in Western Christianity call the sacraments.

Our Catholic approach to the understanding of sacraments identifies two ways to understand these mysteries of God: the seven sacraments, and the broader sense of sacramentality. The seven sacraments — baptism, confirmation, Eucharist, reconciliation, matrimony, holy orders, and the anointing of the sick — provide divinely instituted avenues of grace that allow us to be reborn in Christ, strengthened in Christ, fed by Christ, forgiven in Christ, commissioned by Christ, and healed by Christ.

Each sacrament provides an opportunity to receive God's grace, with the Eucharist as the Sacrament of Sacraments in which Christ is really and truly present in his Body, Blood, Soul, and Divinity. In the transformation of bread and wine into the Body and Blood of Christ and through the reception of Christ in the Eucharist, we see an opportunity for us to be slowly transformed into another expression of God's love in the world. The Eucharist gives us Jesus as our living bread, our food for the journey, and allows us to grow in our citizenship in the kingdom of God.

From the seven sacraments flows the broader sense of seeing our world through sacramental eyes. Jesus is the center of human history and our source and summit. Therefore, all things flow from God through Christ, and all things return to God through Christ. This is why Catholics have sacred reminders and relics called sacramentals. These objects are not the sacraments, but they point us toward Christ's presence in the sacraments.

This appreciation of sacramentals and the broader sacramental world view points us

Scripture

Genesis 1:28–31

God blessed them and God said to them: Be fertile and multiply; fill the earth and subdue it. Have dominion over the fish of the sea, the birds of the air, and all the living things that crawl on the earth.

God also said: See, I give you every seed-bearing plant on all the earth and every tree that has seed-bearing fruit on it to be your food; and to all the wild animals, all the birds of the air, and all the living creatures that crawl on the earth, I give all the green plants for food. And so it happened.

God looked at everything he had made, and found it very good. Evening came, and morning followed — the sixth day.

Job 38:4–15

Where were you when I founded the earth?
Tell me, if you have understanding.
Who determined its size? Surely you know?
Who stretched out the measuring line for it?
Into what were its pedestals sunk,
and who laid its cornerstone,
While the morning stars sang together
and all the sons of God shouted for joy?
Who shut within doors the sea,
when it burst forth from the womb,
When I made the clouds its garment
and thick darkness its swaddling bands?
When I set limits for it
and fastened the bar of its door,
And said: Thus far shall you come but no farther,
and here shall your proud waves stop?
Have you ever in your lifetime commanded the morning
and shown the dawn its place
For taking hold of the ends of the earth,
till the wicked are shaken from it?
The earth is changed as clay by the seal,
and dyed like a garment;
But from the wicked their light is withheld,
and the arm of pride is shattered.

to one of the most basic understandings of the word *reverence*: to treat holy things in a holy way and to treat God's gifts with love, dignity, and respect. This, ironically, presents a stunning question: If God created all things and we are asked to treat God's creation with love, dignity, and respect, what in creation doesn't contain at least a hint of sacramentality? This insight then presents the healthiest definition of sin: a privation or lack of the good. Evil is not a "thing" with flesh and bones, but the absence of goodness, and is embraced by those of flesh and bone who ignore their inherent goodness and the gift of the world around them.

I often come back to these reflections on a personal level when attending the ACME workshops. The Jesuits of the Vatican Observatory throw us into the world of professional astronomy and intuitively introduce us to a sacramental worldview of our cosmos. Yes, that cosmos contains violent explosions, destruction, and death we could see as "natural evil." However, it also presents to us new life, a means of "seeding" our earth to allow God to bring forth the gift of life, the gift of you and the gift of me. We possess an intuitive sense that this world is moving toward something, an end of one sort or another. The

problem is that this end can at times seem to lack clarity and raises the understandable question: Where is this all going?

One of the more controversial figures in modern Catholic thought is the Jesuit Teilhard de Chardin. In his writings, he sought to develop a new metaphysics in light of modern science. Metaphysics, in very basic terms, deals with questions of what it means to exist, what is the relationship between our body and soul, what is our purpose, and how does God relate to the world.

Chardin developed the principle of a type of spiritual "evolution" where the human person and all of creation is moving from matter to spirit. His work is rather dense and complex, but for the purpose of this reflection, it's safe to say his ideas were problematic for the Catholic Church. However, on July 24, 2009, Pope Benedict XVI offered a homily that reintroduced Chardin's thought in a surprising and accessible way. The traditional-minded Benedict drew upon the progressive, often problematic vision of Chardin to re-present his "matter evolving to spirit" theology in a deeply sacramental manner:

> We ourselves, with our whole being, must be adoration and sacrifice, and by transforming our world, give it back to God. The role of the priesthood is to consecrate the world so that it may become a living host, a liturgy: so that the liturgy may not be something alongside the reality of the world, but that the world itself shall become a living host, a liturgy. This is also the great vision of Teilhard de Chardin: in the end we shall achieve a true cosmic liturgy, where the cosmos becomes a living host. And let us pray the Lord to help us become priests in this sense, to aid in the transformation of the world, in adoration of God, beginning with ourselves. That our lives may speak of God, that our lives may be a true liturgy, an announcement of God, a door through which the distant God may become the present God, and a true giving of ourselves to God.

Though Benedict XVI did not use this term, his homily hints at a type of "transubstantiation of the cosmos," in which all of creation returns to and is renewed by its Source and Summit. Benedict takes our understanding of how the Eucharist transforms us and extends it to the theology of the New Jerusalem — the kingdom of God fully revealed, an apocalyptic recreation not rooted in fear, destruction, and violence, but an apocalypse of love and perfection through God's grace.

When we connect this chapter to our previous chapter on the *ordo* of creation and natural liturgy, a sacramental worldview forms that does not treat these natural liturgical moments as mere "happy accidents" but as moments of grace that can stir our hearts and bring creation to true transformation through God's love and grace. Sadly, sin is also present in our world, and the privation of the good can facilitate a regression in our pursuit of God.

Still, a sacramental cosmos and a sacramental worldview call us to a simple but profound disposition of heart: to show reverence to the holy things of God and to give love, dignity, and respect to things made by God's hand.

Spiritual Exercise

This reflection naturally connects with the end of the first creation story of Genesis, when God looks upon the totality of creation and calls it "very good" — or, more accurate to the Hebrew, "good good." Can you see this goodness in the world around you? Look around today and pray for eyes to see this goodness — the goodness in your neighbor; the goodness in you. And ask God to keep your heart far from sin and to help you seek reconciliation when you stray. Desire to be transformed into an expression of God's love in the world.

— 10 —

A Timeless Universe

What is time? Does time even exist? What does it mean to have a beginning and an end? No, I'm not trying to drag you through the introduction to philosophy course that drove you crazy. Instead, I'm presenting basic questions with complex answers.

First, what does time mean to you? Most modern societies place high priority on the idea of "timeliness": We have a place to be and a thing to do, and only a limited amount of time to do it in. This mentality toward time helps people feel productive — achieving a goal through the gift of time.

Though timeliness is important, we also know that only living life with a productive mindset presents several challenges. How many marriages have faced grave difficulties because the time given to one's professional life was skewed in proportion to the time given to one's spouse? How many people experience an inner emptiness after achieving a great many things, but still feel something more fundamental is needed? These moments can lead to the realization that we give time to our work lives, but do we make and give time to ourselves and each other?

These questions lead to a different type of time we need to experience in our lives: wasted time. This term is meant to be a bit tongue-in-cheek, since I draw this from a complaint I hear from people about the Mass: "Father, Mass is waste of time!"

What is wasted time, and is the Mass wasted time? If by wasting time you mean doing something where productivity is not the goal, and the time given to tasks is rather fluid with no real beginning or end and doesn't seek a utilitarian end, then absolutely, Mass is a waste of time!

However, wouldn't we need to affirm that love is a waste of time as well? Love isn't defined by a set beginning or end. In fact, some of the healthiest marriages I know answer the question, "When did the two of you know you wanted to marry each other?"

with the response, "There wasn't a distinct moment — it was revealed to both of us over time."

These different senses of time are referred to in faith as the ordinary passing of time (*Chronos*) and timeless moments or, to borrow an often-used phrase, "when time stands still" (*Kyros*).

Another way to make this distinction is to identify time given to the things we do in contrast to time given to deepening and understanding who we are in God's eyes. Things like prayer, the Mass, sharing time with a loved one, or being wrapped in joy with something that makes us lose our sense of time are expressions of the timeless Kyros, while our jobs, travel, and functional aspects of life are the marked time of Chronos.

Ironically, this fluid sense of time is an overlap between faith and science. As I write, the best science of the first part of the twenty-first century sees time as a bit of an illusion or a human construct. What we perceive as the passing of time is often the

Scripture

Ecclesiastes 3:11

God has made everything appropriate to its time, but has put the timeless into their hearts so they cannot find out, from beginning to end, the work which God has done.

2 Corinthians 4:16–18

We are not discouraged; rather, although our outer self is wasting away, our inner self is being renewed day by day. For this momentary light affliction is producing for us an eternal weight of glory beyond all comparison, as we look not to what is seen but to what is unseen; for what is seen is transitory, but what is unseen is eternal.

1 Peter 1:3–7

Blessed be the God and Father of our Lord Jesus Christ, who in his great mercy gave us a new birth to a living hope through the resurrection of Jesus Christ from the dead, to an inheritance that is imperishable, undefiled, and unfading, kept in heaven for you who by the power of God are safeguarded through faith, to a salvation that is ready to be revealed in the final time.

In this you rejoice, although now for a little while you may have to suffer through various trials, so that the genuineness of your faith, more precious than gold that is perishable even though tested by fire, may prove to be for praise, glory, and honor at the revelation of Jesus Christ.

observation of decay and the change that comes through that decay. I've sometimes wondered if this sense of time might be behind why many who are older feel that time moves faster than when they were young.

Believe it or not, faith also has a fluid sense of time. We have already explored the difference between Chronos and Kryos, but Saint Augustine wonders in his *Confessions* if time isn't what we think it to be. Perhaps time is simply a measurement of change:

> For what is time? Who can readily and briefly explain this? Who can even in thought comprehend it, so as to utter a word about it? But what in discourse do we mention more familiarly and knowingly, than time? And, we understand, when we speak of it; we understand also, when we hear it spoken of by another. What then is time? If no one asks me, I know: if I wish to explain it to one that asketh, I know not: yet I say boldly that I know, that if nothing passed away, time past were not; and if nothing were coming, a time to come were not; and if nothing were, time present were not. Those two times then, past and to come, how are they, seeing the past now is not, and that to come is not yet? But the present, should it always be present, and never pass into time past, verily it should not be time, but eternity. If time present (if it is to be time) only cometh into existence, because it passeth into time past, how can we say that either this is, whose cause of being is, that it shall not be; so, namely, that we cannot truly say that time is, but because it is tending not to be?

This quote is just a small sample of Saint Augustine's reflection on time (for more, read book 11 of the *Confessions.*) Whether it be the mere passing of things in and out of existence or the change we go through as a people as we pursue a relationship with God, Augustine lays out that time may be simply an observation of changes that are a part of God's creative act. It would be a stretch to say that Augustine understood quantum physics before the concept existed, but the idea of time being something more abstract than what we presume is not a new idea. Wrestling with a "new" understanding of time may help us understand more deeply God's creative act and plan for salvation.

Understanding the night sky is a mix of productive time and wasted time. It involves measurements, categories, classifications, and change. Astronomy also involves moments of joy, amazement, wonder, and gratitude for what God has made. The work of astronomy often utilizes tools like telescopes, computers, and cameras, but once those tools are set up and put to work, the astronomer is blessed with time for prayer, contemplation, and conversation with God and/or another as he waits for the tools to finish their job.

Spiritual Exercise

It's time to put this book down and plan some time for observation. Let's see if we can give you a simple example of the work and contemplation of astronomy. Most of us have some type of smart phone with a camera on it. Most of these phones will have a "night mode" or some kind of setting to help you take a longer exposure of the sky. Go out on a clear night, set your phone to night mode, and try to take a picture of the night sky.

For this exercise, don't worry about trying to take a picture of specific parts of the sky. Instead, just play a little and take images until you have one where you can see stars. Zoom in on the image. How many stars can you see? Then simply look at the night sky with your naked eye. How many stars can you see now? What colors do you see in the night sky? Do you see blue, orange, red, yellow, white, or other colors? What colors dominate the night sky? Explore these questions, study what these questions invite you to contemplate, and waste a little time just gazing into God's creation. It's true that we all need both productive time and nonproductive, life-giving timelessness. Try on a clear night to discover a little bit of both.

– 11 –

The Curse of Certitude

Since I began writing for *The Catholic Astronomer*, I have had to address many misconceptions about my relationship with the Vatican Observatory. Many times, people presume that I am a Vatican scientist (I am not). Others presume that I am a professional scientist turned priest (nope). Some presume that I have an advanced degree in cosmology or hold a university position (wrong again). As I shared in the introduction to this book, I'm simply a diocesan priest who also has a deep interest in and passion for science, especially astronomy.

So, why am I interested in science if this isn't a central part of my priestly ministry? The lighthearted answer I often give is that I have always cared about things that people find less interesting. The more accurate answer is both simple and challenging: The sciences inspire me to be a better priest.

One of the reasons I love science is that it feeds my desire to explore and embark on adventures. When I read pieces from NASA about the Cassini Mission to Saturn, see Juno Cam images of Jupiter, marvel at the images from the New Horizons' flyby of Pluto, watch as the European Space Agency (ESA) lands a probe on a comet with the Rosetta Mission, and visit fascinating places like the Steward Observatory Mirror Lab on the campus of the University of Arizona, I am inspired to explore my faith in a deeper way, just as science explores the mysteries of the natural world in new and deeper ways.

Something I think science (astronomy in particular) captures, which religion is quickly losing, is the idea of limitless exploration, motivated by a profound sense of awe and wonder. During one of my visits to OSIRIS-REx, I asked the following question of one of the mission scientists, Carl Hergenroth: "If there were no limits placed upon the exploration of space, where would you go?" His answer was quick and direct: "The deepest known parts of the universe." His clear, confident response resonated deeply within me, inspiring me to have the same confidence to delve into my understanding of the natural

CHURCH

Scripture

Hebrews 11:1–3
Faith is the realization of what is hoped for and evidence of things not seen. Because of it the ancients were well attested. By faith we understand that the universe was ordered by the word of God, so that what is visible came into being through the invisible.

1 Peter 1:6–12
In this you rejoice, although now for a little while you may have to suffer through various trials, so that the genuineness of your faith, more precious than gold that is perishable even though tested by fire, may prove to be for praise, glory, and honor at the revelation of Jesus Christ.

Although you have not seen him you love him; even though you do not see him now yet believe in him, you rejoice with an indescribable and glorious joy, as you attain the goal of [your] faith, the salvation of your souls.

Concerning this salvation, prophets who prophesied about the grace that was to be yours searched and investigated it, investigating the time and circumstances that the Spirit of Christ within them indicated when it testified in advance to the sufferings destined for Christ and the glories to follow them.

It was revealed to them that they were serving not themselves but you with regard to the things that have now been announced to you by those who preached the good news to you [through] the holy Spirit sent from heaven, things into which angels longed to look.

world and also to explore the depths of who I am in God's eyes.

I think theology can learn from science that there is an inspirational ethos which can be created when something like faith is not merely approached as an intellectual discipline to be understood, but as an adventure to be lived and explored with deep passion. When theology delves so deep into the language of professional academia that it no longer speaks to or inspires the layperson in the pew, it can become a dead letter with little practical application. Granted, some of the most advanced science can be dizzying to even the most articulate in their given field, but a good scientist can find a way to make these realities accessible to the public — even if they are poorly understood.

Yes, we need high intellects in the Church to further the academic exploration of theology. However, we also need voices in the pastoral field who can take the complexity of the scholar and present it to the people of faith in a way that inspires them to embrace an adventure of faith, hope, and love.

Unfortunately, I often see a deficiency in this overly systematic approach to theology.

All too often, I encounter a bland faith of practicality in which adventure is lost, replaced with paying bills, developing programs, and keeping tabs on the number of parishioners in the pews. My fear is that faith is becoming so pragmatic that even the idea of pilgrimage, a sacred journey, is being dropped in favor of pressing play on the DVD player to watch the latest series on catechetical instruction. Put another way, I fear that we are living in the midst of "living room Catholicism."

Now, someone might rightfully object that I am over-glamorizing the sciences and emphasize that the daily routine of most scientists involves staring at a computer screen for hours on end with little sense of adventure and exploration. True, but the point I wish to make is that science is never afraid to explore a new frontier, ask a harder question than was asked before, or insist on precise answers to life's deepest questions. Do we have the same disposition of heart when we approach our faith life? Or are we more comfortable with the simple, lukewarm attitude of "Just be nice, and that's enough"?

Lukewarmness doesn't square with Jesus' call for us to be either hot or cold (see Rv 3:16). Nor does it square with science when, even after a new discovery is made, established truths are tested repeatedly to see if there is something new to be learned or if the original premise was true in the first place.

This revisiting of known truths reminds me of the heart of Ignatian prayer, which invites us to pore over the same Scripture passage time and time again to deepen our understanding of the text. When was the last time you decided to pray with one passage for an entire week to try and deepen your understanding of the Bible? How often have we read one passage from the Bible and simply presumed that the first reading was enough and there was nothing more to learn? Again, I think science can go a long way in helping us deepen our faith, enriching it through a desire to delve deeper and deeper into the mystery of our created world.

Does your faith allow for the possibility of adventure? Do you see a potential bridge between faith and science in the willingness to explore new ideas and possibilities in a limitless manner? Has our faith become far too pragmatic for its own good? Pray with these questions. Through such prayer, inspired by the adventurous heart of scientific exploration, we can breathe new life into our faith.

One of the dangers when trying to live the spiritual life is presuming that having *certain faith* requires us to have no room for doubt. This is an error for a number of reasons, the foremost being that the very term "certain faith" is a paradox. The word *certain* implies a level of completion while *faith* implies the lack of a full understanding of God which still embraces God's love. It is this "lack" that sparks the seeker of God to grow closer to him through prayerful and intellectual investigation. Put another way, we can have certain faith but still have questions about God. The two are not mutually exclusive.

The study of the night sky evokes a level of faith. Consider the study of "dark matter" and "dark energy." Dark matter has a "drawing together" property, and dark energy has a "pushing apart" property. What are dark matter and dark energy? We don't know. We can observe phenomena that clearly indicate something is impacting our universe, but we can't define or identify what that something is. We have faith that there is something to discover, which we named dark matter and dark energy, but we still don't completely understand what these realities are.

What happens in faith and in science when our belief encounters moments when what we know to be true commingles with things that confuse, and we can't explain it? Does our lack of understanding lead us to a deflating doubt, to presuming that if we can't understand something completely, we can't have belief? Or do we have the heart of a scientist that sees those moments as the starting point of exploration? Do we see those moments as the reason to embark on a journey of deepening our understanding, or as the end of the journey?

Spiritual Exercise

Gaze into the night sky long enough, and I guarantee that you will see and experience things you don't understand. Are you content with not knowing, or will those moments inspire you to explore? Look into your life of faith long enough, and I guarantee that there will be things you will not understand about yourself and God. Are you content with not knowing yourself and God, or will those moments inspire you to explore?

— 12 —

God Rewards Perseverance

From time to time people will ask me, "Father James, what should I do if I want to get into astronomy or astrophotography?" The answer to this question is more complicated than one may think. If the person asking the question simply wants to go out on a clear night occasionally, I can easily encourage him or her to get a nice pair of binoculars and find constellations and easier targets in the night sky. If he or she wants to do more serious observing or astrophotography that involves a deeper commitment to the time needed to observe, I ask an important question:

"How important is a good night's sleep to you?"

If the answer is, "It's of high importance," then my reply would be, "Just be an enthusiast."

There's a simple axiom in hobby astronomy that needs to be embraced: "You can't see it unless you're out looking for it." Astronomy requires time, patience, a bit of a learning curve, and more time and more patience. If we don't take that time, we will miss out on the wonders of the night.

There have been times in my love of astronomy when I have struggled a bit with the motivation to be out. A good example of that is the experiences I've had with the northern lights. In the past, I've always struggled to see the northern lights, also known as Aurora Borealis — a phenomenon that occurs when solar winds from the sun interact with the Earth's atmosphere. The solar winds are a product of a solar storm on the sun that is pointed straight at the Earth. It takes some time for the solar winds from those eruptions to reach the Earth, depending on the intensity of the explosion. The strength of these explosions also plays into how intense the aurora will be.

As of the time of the writing of this book, the sun has been in what is called "solar maximum." The sun goes through twelve-year cycles, with twelve years of a lot of solar storms, and then twelve years of minimal solar storms. Currently, science doesn't have a

complete understanding of why the sun goes through such cycles, but when we are in a time of solar maximum, the chance of seeing the northern lights is much better.

The first night I truly beheld the northern lights in all their glory was in the winter of 2024. I was tempted that evening not to go out and look for this phenomenon, since I was rather exhausted. My bishop at the time, Bishop Callahan, had asked me to celebrate three Confirmation Masses over two days for him. Having finished the first of these three Masses, my body told me to go to bed. Yes, I heard all day from friends that the northern lights were going to be spectacular. Still, I felt the need to pace myself with the heavier-than-usual workload.

As I was winding down for the evening, I decided to check social media. The first post that showed up on my newsfeed was from my uncle, Jeff Kurzynski:

"Just look up! Go outside and just look up!"

This simple and direct post was accompanied by his images of the aurora. "Wow!" I uttered under my breath. What was my next thought?

"If I'm going to do this, I'm going to do it right."

I grabbed my camera, a couple of lenses, and my tripod and made my way out of town for about twenty minutes. I was very, very happy that I hadn't listened to my inner common sense. I let my love of the night sky rule my decisions that evening and into morning, and I was rewarded. I saw ribbons of light green and red dancing through the night sky. At one point, a woman in a car drove up to me and asked, "Where are the northern lights?"

"Look up, they're all around you!" I responded.

She looked out of her car window and simply said, "No, those are just clouds. I'm

Scripture

Psalm 19:1

The heavens declare the glory of God; the firmament proclaims the works of his hands.

Psalm 24:8–9

Who is this king of glory?
The LORD, strong and mighty,
the LORD, mighty in war.
Lift up your heads, O gates;
rise up, you ancient portals,
that the king of glory may enter.

Isaiah 66:1–2

The heavens are my throne,
the earth, my footstool.
What house can you build for me?
Where is the place of my rest?
My hand made all these things
when all of them came to be.

Luke 11:5–8

And he said to them, "Suppose one of you has a friend to whom he goes at midnight and says, 'Friend, lend me three loaves of bread, for a friend of mine has arrived at my house from a journey and I have nothing to offer him,' and he says in reply from within, 'Do not bother me; the door has already been locked and my children and I are already in bed. I cannot get up to give you anything.'

I tell you, if he does not get up to give him the loaves because of their friendship, he will get up to give him whatever he needs because of his persistence."

going home."

I wanted to show her some of the pictures I was taking, but she drove off before I could make the offer. The greens and reds appeared far stronger on my camera, given its ability to do longer exposures and capture more light, and I was able to view more than with the naked eye.

Selfishly, my feelings of regret for her decision left quickly as I had the sky to myself, simply watching the celestial dance occur. Under those ribbons of light, I experienced peace, wonder, joy, and decompression from the work I had done. The movements of the northern lights had such a playful character that I felt as if God were inviting me to participate in the game.

My experience of the northern lights also reminded me of a quote from the naturalist John Muir. Though originally from Scotland, Muir is a bit of a naturalist hero where I live in Wisconsin. Muir wrote openly about his struggles with faith, growing up in a strict Calvinist home that was, at times, abusive. Still, Muir retained very positive and loving memories of his father and would speak of faith, even in his struggles, that was very Catholic in its intuition.

Muir wrote about his first experience with the northern lights when his family immigrated to Wisconsin. He expresses exhilaration and almost apocalyptic wonder at the glory he experienced watching these lights:

> The winter stars far surpassed those of our stormy Scotland in brightness, and we gazed and gazed as though we had never seen stars before. Oftentimes the heavens were made still more glorious by auroras, the long lance rays, called "Merry Dancers" in Scotland, streaming with startling tremulous motion to the zenith. Usually the electric auroral light is white or pale yellow, but in the third or fourth of our Wisconsin winters there was a magnificently colored aurora that was seen and admired over nearly all the continent. The whole sky was draped in gracious purple and crimson folds glorious beyond description. Father called us out into the yard in front of the house where he had a wide view, crying, "Come! Come, mother! Come, bairns! and see the glory of God. All the sky is clad in a robe of red light. Look straight up to the crown where the folds are gathered. Hush and wonder and adore, for surely this is the clothing of the Lord Himself, and perhaps He will even now appear looking down from his high heaven." This celestial show was far more glorious than anything we had ever yet beheld, and throughout that wonderful winter hardly anything else was spoken of. (*Natural Writings*)

I can't say for sure, but I speculate that the strong reds he references are a rare phenomenon called "The Forbidden Emission Line." Michelle Thaller, a friend of mine who worked for NASA, explained to me that this occurs when the atmosphere is very still and the oxygen in the upper atmosphere is not disturbed for days, and then the solar winds excite that

oxygen in such a way that it pops with a glorious red color.

Watching the northern lights on another night, I saw that red and was able to capture a very nice image of it. The reference by Muir's father of a "crown where the folds are gathered" was easy for me to imagine when looking at the picture I took. When the Muir family had this powerful experience, it was probably even more striking, given the lower amount of light pollution in the mid 1800s. Still, I felt a moment of spiritual solidarity with Muir's father, beholding the glory of God and sensing that God was looking upon me.

The passion that ACME's workshops helped foster in me also provided motivation to fight through the exhaustion and not to miss both a powerful experience of the night sky and an equally powerful moment of prayer. You can't see it and experience it if you aren't out there looking for it.

Spiritual Exercise

Have you ever experienced the northern lights? If you haven't, I would encourage you to figure out a way to do so. They are rare occurrences, but ones that move the mind and the heart with joy and peace. There are many resources on the internet you can use to get forecasts of when and where the lights may occur.

"Father James, that sounds wonderful, but I struggle to find the motivation to pray — let alone go out into the dark at night to pray with northern lights that can be challenging to see!" To those of you who feel this way, you're in good company! I sometimes find myself lacking the motivation to go out when I feel deep stress and exhaustion sets in. Perhaps you live somewhere that makes it impossible to see the northern lights. Even if you don't have the ability to take yourself somewhere to see them, I encourage you to use the images in this chapter (or others you can find online) to spend a few moments in prayer. Let the beauty of these images be a backdrop for reveling at the wonder of God's creation. Use these images as a type of natural icon, gazing upon them and allowing God to play with your heart as John Muir's father did. When I allow my heart to reflect on God's beauty in creation, even in times of deep exhaustion, it brings great peace to my heart, reminding me that I, too, am a part of God's beautiful creation.

— 13 —

Count the Stars If You Can

As we approach the closing chapters of this book, we return to where we began: gazing into a sky full of stars. Who was the first person to gaze into the night sky in wonder? I would venture to say that just about everyone in human history who was able to see the night sky has done so.

As I shared earlier, stars are often used in the Bible to symbolize people. Even the most famous reference to stars in the Bible, the Star of Bethlehem (which we will consider in more detail in the next chapter), points less to an astronomical event and more to a person who, according to the writings of Isaiah, is light — the light awaited by the people who lived in darkness (see Is 9:1). This is important to remember when we encounter those who spend a great deal of time and energy trying to answer whether

Scripture

Genesis 15:1–6

Some time afterward, the word of the LORD came to Abram in a vision: Do not fear, Abram! I am your shield; I will make your reward very great. But Abram said, "Lord GOD, what can you give me, if I die childless and have only a servant of my household, Eliezer of Damascus?" Abram continued, "Look, you have given me no offspring, so a servant of my household will be my heir." Then the word of the LORD came to him: No, that one will not be your heir; your own offspring will be your heir. He took him outside and said: Look up at the sky and count the stars, if you can. Just so, he added, will your descendants be. Abram put his faith in the LORD, who attributed it to him as an act of righteousness.

or not the Star of Bethlehem was an actual astronomical event. As fascinating as the explorations can be, they can also be a distractive rabbit hole that can draw our attention away from him whom the star signifies.

The next most popular reference to stars in Scripture would be the discourse between God and Abraham. When God establishes his covenant with Abraham, the stars become a powerful teaching tool to express the fruitfulness of the promise God is making: Count the stars if you can. Count the grains of the sand on the beach.

The point is profound and clear: When God makes a promise with us, it will be fruitful beyond anything we can imagine.

I sometimes wonder what Abraham experienced when looking into a sky full of stars, trying to understand what God's covenant really meant. When we take modern astronomy into account, this metaphor of God's covenant is even more striking. In the time of Abraham, the naked eye would strain to count the thousands of visible stars on

a dark night in the Middle East. In our modern times, our astronomical tools reveal the unthinkable trillions of stars and galaxies that are known and unknown, deepening the visual sea of wonder we call the universe. If Abraham were presented with the Hubble and James Webb Telescopes' images of deep space, how much more would he have both understood and been humbled by the extent of God's love for him?

What makes this covenant even more humbling and awe-inspiring is that both you and I are a part of that promise. We participate in the fruitfulness of the covenant, as will those people of faith who will come after us.

For us as Catholics, signs and symbols carry with them a sacramental undercurrent. Every time you see a night sky full of stars, it is a reminder that you are part of God's fruitfulness: You are loved, you are treasured, and in this cosmos of wonder and awe, you are a cosmos of wonder and awe.

Spiritual Exercise

On a clear night, go out to a dark place where you can appreciate the clear night sky. Read Genesis 15, place yourself in Abraham's shoes, and then look up. Try to count the stars if you can. Gaze in wonder at what you see, and see in this sign of the stars a constant reminder of the love God had for Abraham, the love God has for you, and the love God has for every person who has ever existed and will ever exist.

— 14 —

Applying Our Liturgical and Sacramental Vision to Christmas

A reflection on the Catholic vision of the night sky would not be complete without reflecting on most people's favorite astronomy topic: the Star of Bethlehem. There are many approaches, questions, and understandings that one can traverse — some illuminating and awe-inspiring; others simply rabbit holes that create confusion and make us miss the point of what Christmas is supposed to focus upon. This reflection will look at some of these rabbit holes in the hopes of enriching your understanding of the Star of Bethlehem and of Christmas.

For our first rabbit hole, we will explore the question of the actual date of Christ's birth. Some may think that if we look back at star charts, we might be able to confirm a distant "December 25" in the ancient world as Jesus' actual birthday. I wish it were that easy, but sadly, it's a bit more complicated.

To begin with, the first stumbling block we need to overcome is the fact that the Bible doesn't give us a date for Jesus' birth. In fact, only two of the four Gospels even deal with the infancy of Jesus. Therefore, our first question to ask is this: *If the actual date of Jesus' birth was so important, then why didn't all four Gospels have an infancy narrative or strongly emphasize the date when Jesus was born?* Of the many answers that could be given, I find the simplest answer to be that we first need to see the birth of Jesus in light of Jewish culture at that time.

In ancient Jewish culture, one did not celebrate the birth of a child. The Children of Israel were rather hesitant to celebrate a child's birth because that's what the pagans of the

Roman Empire celebrated. Therefore, the culture from which Christianity emerged did not emphasize the celebration of birth.

So, if Jewish custom preferred not to celebrate one's birth, what was the day of significance that was celebrated? In Jewish culture, it was an ancient custom that is now called the *yahrzeit*, or the day of one's death. The modern celebration of the yahrzeit differs slightly from the practices at the time of Jesus, but the essence of the remembrance was that the family would commemorate the death of a loved one each year on the day they had died. Families would light a candle and fast for twenty-four hours to commemorate the day.

I find it a tantalizing parallel that what was seen as of the utmost importance to the early Christians was the celebration of the day Jesus rose from the dead. This commemoration was not remembered with fasting, but with feasting — with what we would call today the Mass. So central was this mystery that it was celebrated every week, not to encourage a "go to Mass or else" mentality, but to celebrate every Sunday as the Day of Resurrection. Therefore, whether it be the candles we light at Mass, the vigil lamp by the tabernacle where the Eucharist is reserved, or a devout mother lighting a votive candle on the anniversary of her son's death, I can't help but see a hint of the ancient practices of Judaism that led to the yahrzeit. This intuition is strengthened by the fact that the celebration of Christmas was a later development and not part of the earliest feasts of the Church. Instead, the day of Christ's Resurrection, offering us the hope of our bodily resurrection to eternal life, was always central to Christian faith.

So, does that mean that the Star of Bethlehem has nothing to do with Jesus' birth? Oh no, on the contrary, the Star of Bethlehem holds great significance! However, it might be in a way that differs from our presumptions.

What I find far more meaningful when exploring questions like the Star of Bethlehem and the date of Christmas are the spiritual and metaphorical interpretations of why Jesus' birthday is celebrated when it is. For example, the date of December 25 is in close relationship to the Jewish feast of Hanukkah, or "the Feast of Lights." In this feast, Jewish families light candles over many nights on a candelabrum called a *menorah* to celebrate the rededication of the Temple. The menorah symbolizes many things, but one of the most basic and applicable is that its candles signify divine light.

When I think of divine light in the biblical sense, I not only think of the Star of Bethlehem, but also of one of the most anticipated lights referenced in the Book of Isaiah:

> The people who walked in darkness
> have seen a great light;
> Upon those who lived in a land of gloom
> a light has shone. (9:1)

To further this connection, Joseph Cardinal Ratzinger, in his book *The Spirit of the Liturgy*, explains how the birth of Jesus is celebrated at about the time of the Winter Solstice when the days are shortest and the nights are longest. After Christmas, however, the days eventually begin to lengthen, pointing to the hope of Easter's Spring and new life. The symbolic significance of this "cosmic liturgy" is that creation is showing us that, when Christ enters the world, the light overcomes the darkness. (Of course, this interpretation only works in the Northern Hemisphere.)

Another rabbit hole we can approach is to ask a question that is specific to the Feast of the Epiphany and the Magi. As the classic Christmas passage goes, the Magi from the East encounter Herod and tell him about this new star they are following (see Mt 2:1-12). If Christmas cards were accurate, we could presume the star was some type of ancient flood

Scripture

We have reflected on many things in this chapter, exploring the different approaches we can have to the Star of Bethlehem. Perhaps the best way to approach this topic is to have the humble hearts of the shepherds who were the first people invited to meet the infant Christ, the Light of the World. Use this and your other favorite infancy narratives to develop a sincere and authentic closeness to Christ this Christmas. Let Jesus be the light in your darkness. And may he continue to be, for all of us, the Light of the World.

Luke 2:8–14

Now there were shepherds in that region
living in the fields and keeping the night watch over their flock.
The angel of the Lord appeared to them
and the glory of the Lord shone around them,
and they were struck with great fear.
The angel said to them, "Do not be afraid;
for behold, I proclaim to you good news of great joy
that will be for all the people.
For today in the city of David
a savior has been born for you
who is Messiah and Lord.
And this will be a sign for you:
you will find an infant wrapped in swaddling clothes
and lying in a manger."
And suddenly there was a multitude of the heavenly host with the angel,
praising God and saying:
"Glory to God in the highest
and on earth peace
to those on whom his favor rests."

light in the sky leading the Magi. During the Christmas season of 2024 leading into 2025, we were treated in the night sky to a beautiful conjunction of a thin, crescent moon and Saturn. In the twilight, the close proximity of these two bright objects was stunning! If this conjunction were an accurate parallel to the Star of Bethlehem in terms of visual prominence, I think it safe to say that Herod would have seen the star too. He might not have known what it symbolized, but it would have been rather evident to everyone, including him. Yet, Herod's awareness of the star in Scripture communicates, at best, a vagueness about this event. So, why couldn't Herod see something that should have been rather obvious?

Stars in the Bible do not point out zodiacal events, but they often do signify people or angels. There's even a certain playfulness in how stars are presented in the Bible. The Magi from the East were most likely members of mystery religions that did look to the movements of the stars to find meaning in their lives. The story of the Magi may well be included in the Gospel, at least in part, to show Christ's mission to those who represent "the East" in a spiritual sense. In this way, the story communicates, "You seek truth in the stars, but the light you seek is really a person, an infant, a priest, a prophet and king — the infant Christ."

Perhaps Herod could not see the star, not because he was ignorant of star charts, but because of his disregard for any truth outside of maintaining his sense of power. Perhaps his blindness to the star symbolizes the way he viewed the true "light in the darkness" — Jesus Christ — simply as a threat to his rule instead of something to celebrate. With the blinders of power, prestige, and wealth upon him, Herod lived with his spiritual eyes in the fog, unable to see the light of truth even as it lay in a manger in Bethlehem.

If we take this approach to the star, we can begin to see that all of us, myself included, can fall into the trap of the blindness of Herod. All of us can allow the trappings of power, prestige, and wealth to dim our vision and make seeking the truth of Christ difficult or borderline impossible. Therefore, the heart of the Star of Bethlehem might be a call to detach ourselves from the distractions we spiritually trip on in the darkness and allow the light of faith, hope, and love to illuminate our very being.

So, how do we see with the eyes of faith? In his *Spiritual Exercises*, Saint Ignatius introduces his "Principle and Foundation," wherein he speaks of a disposition of heart called *spiritual indifference*:

> Man was created for a certain end. This end is to praise, to reverence and to serve the Lord his God and by this means to arrive at eternal salvation. All the other beings and objects that surround us on the earth were created for the benefit of man and to be useful to him, as means to his final end; hence his obligation to use, or to abstain from the use of, these creatures, according as they bring him nearer to that end, or tend to separate him from it. Hence we must above all endeavor to establish in ourselves a complete indifference toward all created things, though the use of them may not be otherwise forbidden; not giving, as far as depends on us, any preference to health over sickness, riches over poverty, honor over

> humiliation, a long life over a short. But we must desire and choose definitively in everything what will lead us to the end of our creation. (23)

What this means is that we are to be indifferent to all things in life except for those that draw us closer to Christ. This presumes a time of reflection in order to become aware of the things that draw us closer to Christ and the things that can distract us.

Does this mean that we should not consider the Star of Bethlehem as an historical event and just reflect on its metaphorical significance? No, I don't see a need to swing from one extreme to the other. Br. Guy Consolmagno has shared on a number of occasions that the problem with finding an historical candidate for the Star of Bethlehem isn't that we can't find potential explanations in the night sky at the time of Jesus, but that there are too many candidates when we look back at what the sky was doing in ancient times. Therefore, I would still encourage you to look to the night sky around Christmas.

Personally, I'll never forget a Christmas Eve night back in 1996 when I was in college, halfway through my second senior year at the University of Wisconsin – Stevens Point.

I was home for Christmas, and I remember waking up in the middle of the night; wide awake, I knew that I wasn't going to be able to get back to sleep for a while. Quietly, I walked through my parents' house, hoping not to wake anyone. As I looked out the kitchen windows, I was struck by how bright it was outside, a result of the light from a full moon and its reflection off the snow.

I decided to slip on my coat and boots and go outside to look at the moon for a while. The moon was beautiful, and the night was still and silent. I remember just leaning on the railing of our deck, looking across the fields of our Central Wisconsin farm. I was struck by how the moon made things so bright that it almost felt like day. Suddenly, I heard something off in the distance briefly cry out, breaking the silence (probably a fox). The cry echoed through the night like the harmonious resolution of a choir that arrives at the final cadence of a motet.

Something grabbed my emotions in that moment and prompted me to ask, "Was that what it was like to hear the sound of the distant cries of Jesus the night he was born?" My heart rested in peace, and I stayed outside as long as my body would allow me before the cold forced me back inside. I will never forget that mystical night!

Spiritual Exercise

How should we pray with the Star of Bethlehem as an aid for us? Our goal should be, as Saint Ignatius teaches, to cling to an understanding of the Star that brings us closer to Christ instead of one that distracts us from God's love. Perhaps on Christmas Eve, weather permitting depending on where you live, you may simply want to drink in the beauty of the night and ask God in prayer, "What was it like the night that Jesus was born?"

– 15 –

Applying our Liturgical and Sacramental Vision to Easter

The Easter Triduum is the liturgical high point of the year for a Christian. To share an analogy from American football, it's the "Super Bowl of Catholicism." The celebration spans three days: Holy Thursday, Good Friday, and Holy Saturday, or the Easter Vigil. Though these are three separate events, liturgically they are to be seen as one continuous celebration. In a liturgical sense, we enter into timelessness (Kyros) and are present again, as we are every Sunday, to Jesus' life, death, and resurrection.

When I was an altar server in my childhood, we were instructed to ring the bells throughout the sung Gloria on Holy Thursday. After this sung prayer of praise and thanksgiving was done, no bells were to be rung again until the Easter Vigil. At my first assignment, the pastor took this one step further by not having the church bell toll the hours from Thursday to Saturday evening. As a newly ordained priest, I grew to look forward to this silence, and it made me feel like my world had stopped in prayerful contemplation.

I would so look forward to the Easter Triduum in my first years of priesthood. I enjoyed stumbling around the annual question from parishioners, "Father James, what is the date of Easter this year?" As all of us know, Easter is a moving target on the calendar. Hobby astronomer that I am, I was always excited to explain that Easter Sunday would occur on the first Sunday after the first full moon after the spring equinox. It wouldn't surprise me if many of you reading this already knew about this supposed astronomical factoid. The awkward fact is that I later found out at ACME that this really isn't how the date of Easter is determined. Still, most years the formula works, and it's fun to interest my

parishioners in the movements of the night sky at Easter.

As time went on in my priestly ministry, some of that wonder of the Triduum began to wear off. The three holy days became more about planning, planning, and more planning. The prayerful part of Easter began to subside, and, in its place, stress took over Easter. Then, it happened. The most memorable Triduum of my priesthood: Holy Week during the COVID-19 shutdown.

In the spring of 2020, I was scheduled to do a three-month sabbatical at the Redemptorist Renewal Center, just north of Tucson, Arizona. It's the same retreat center that the Vatican Observatory uses for their biannual workshops. As I was preparing to leave for sabbatical, I was worried. My worry wasn't about this "new flu" that I was hearing rumblings about. The fear was that this was going to be the first year in my priesthood that I wouldn't be home for the Easter Triduum.

As the date for my sabbatical fast approached, the Diocese of La Crosse began to send out these cryptic emails about making sure our parishioners washed their hands before distributing Communion because of this new coronavirus. I remember reading that announcement at the final Mass before I left for sabbatical. I asked the parishioner who was driving me to the airport, "Mike, do you think that announcement I made was a bit odd?"

I arrived in Tucson and, one week later, the global shutdown began. Needless to say, it impacted my experience of sabbatical. I felt confused and scared, and I wanted to go back home so I could be with my parish through all of this, but I couldn't. Then I heard that Masses were shut down until further notice. One week, and the world literally came to a screaming halt.

Suddenly, my first Triduum away from the parish didn't mean that much to me. Yes, Masses were still celebrated, and we all learned how to do livestreaming on the fly, but the overarching concerns for all of us were more basic: Is this the "new normal"? If my loved ones get sick, will I ever see them again? Will I be able to get back to Wisconsin while I'm in Arizona during the shutdown? It's a time of our lives that we all would rather forget. However, avoidance of a painful past only creates issues for us later on. We all need to come to terms with the reality that the world stood in silent emotional and spiritual trauma. The world was experiencing Good Friday, collectively crying out, "My God, My God, why have you forsaken me?"

During that time, I wrote this prayer as a part of my Holy Week in Arizona:

Mary,
You were called to protect Jesus during the most vulnerable years of his life.
You loved him, nurtured him, and
taught him to walk, speak, and pray.
You laughed with him in times of joy,
cried with him in times of distress,
ministered to him when he was sick,
and consoled him when he was rejected.

You were mother to him and needed to be his mother,
assisting Jesus to grow and embrace his earthly mission.

Mary, we call upon your loving presence in this time of crisis.
Under the title of "Our Lady of Perpetual Help,"
we are reminded of a gentle embrace between a mother and her child,
the embrace you shared with Jesus.
May this image of maternal care become a reality for those who are in isolation,
whether they are ill or experience fear of illness.

For those who will see the veil fall between time and eternity through death,
may your prayers comfort and encourage them,
leading them to discover new life with your Son, Jesus Christ,
just as an infant finds his family for the first time through birth.

Mary, for those who will perish today
without the loving touch of family or friends to comfort them,
fill the hospital rooms, nursing homes, and beds that hold the sick and dying
with the warmth of your maternal embrace.

Where hands are reaching for someone to love them in their suffering,
grasp them and wrap them in your mantle of love and protection.
Be with them in their solitude now and at the hour of their death,
placing their hand in the hand of Jesus.
Give them courage to walk with him from time to eternity.
We ask this through Christ our Lord.
Amen.

Our Lady of Perpetual Help, pray for us.

As Easter approached, the full moon after the spring equinox was of little interest to me. Instead, I found the scriptural references to the sun turning dark far more impactful. We all were living a Good Friday. I think it safe to say that many of us were beginning to wonder if there would be an Easter Sunday of hope.

During that Holy Week, I took a walk into what is called "the wash" at the Renewal Center. It's a dried river bed behind the center that floods during the rainy season. I wanted to get a nice image of the stars, but I also wanted an interesting foreground image. Then, I saw it — a dead cactus that, with the stars as its backdrop, looked like a crucifix in the desert. While my camera was taking images of the dead cactus, I could feel the hymn "Were You There?" quietly echoing in my prayer. That cactus became an image of Good Friday and the COVID-19 shutdown for me that year — the commingling of death, ugliness, beauty, and salvation.

Thankfully, as I hope we all have experienced, Easter Sunday did come for our world. We emerged from shutdown, and began to get our lives back together again. I do wonder at times if we really have faced what we went through in a redemptive way, trying to find God's grace in that time of difficulty. I suppose the answer to that question is quite personal for each one of us, but I pray that we can continue to heal from that Good Friday experience.

Lunar cycles, spring equinoxes, darkened suns, a dead star-lit cactus, and an empty tomb of hope … yes, I believe that does summarize my sabbatical experience quite well. And it also reminds me that sometimes the symbols of our faith are universal and other times quite personal. Though we all can learn the mostly accurate way to date Easter with the night sky, those same skies may yield a personal encounter with God in either struggle or joy.

Since then, my joy in the Easter Triduum has returned. The waiting for sundown to begin the Holy Saturday Vigil has recaptured its wonder. The Easter Candle that signifies the light of Christ illuminating the darkness of the world speaks to me again. And when I am done with Holy Saturday, if the skies are clear, I will often stop during my walk back to the rectory, gaze into the night sky, and thank God that in the silence of that evening, hope has risen like the sunrise. Jesus Christ is risen from the dead!

Spiritual Exercise

To help apply our liturgical and sacramental perspective to Easter, take some time on a clear night and pray with the text of the Easter Exultet. It is an ancient hymn that, when sung in the low candlelight of the Easter Vigil, can evoke deep peace which reflects the wonder of that holy night. And when you face a Good Friday in your life, allow these words and a gaze into a night sky full of stars to give you the confidence that dawn is coming, the Son has risen, and hope will shine forth like the rising sun.

The Exultet

Exult, let them exult, the hosts of heaven,
exult, let Angel ministers of God exult,
let the trumpet of salvation
sound aloud our mighty King's triumph!
Be glad, let earth be glad, as glory floods her,
ablaze with light from her eternal King,
let all corners of the earth be glad,
knowing an end to gloom and darkness.
Rejoice, let Mother Church also rejoice,
arrayed with the lightning of his glory,
let this holy building shake with joy,
filled with the mighty voices of the peoples.
(Therefore, dearest friends,
standing in the awesome glory of this holy light,
invoke with me, I ask you,
the mercy of God almighty,
that he, who has been pleased to number me,
though unworthy, among the Levites,
may pour into me his light unshadowed,
that I may sing this candle's perfect praises.)
(V. The Lord be with you.
R. And with your spirit.)
V. Lift up your hearts.
R. We lift them up to the Lord.
V. Let us give thanks to the Lord our God.
R. It is right and just.
It is truly right and just,
with ardent love of mind and heart
and with devoted service of our voice,
to acclaim our God invisible, the almighty Father,
and Jesus Christ, our Lord, his Son, his Only Begotten.
Who for our sake paid Adam's debt to the eternal Father,
and, pouring out his own dear Blood,
wiped clean the record of our ancient sinfulness.
These, then, are the feasts of Passover,
in which is slain the Lamb, the one true Lamb,
whose Blood anoints the doorposts of

believers.
This is the night,
when once you led our forebears, Israel's children,
from slavery in Egypt
and made them pass dry-shod through the Red Sea.
This is the night
that with a pillar of fire
banished the darkness of sin.
This is the night
that even now, throughout the world,
sets Christian believers apart from worldly vices
and from the gloom of sin,
leading them to grace
and joining them to his holy ones.
This is the night,
when Christ broke the prison-bars of death
and rose victorious from the underworld.
Our birth would have been no gain,
had we not been redeemed.
O wonder of your humble care for us!
O love, O charity beyond all telling,
to ransom a slave you gave away your Son!
O truly necessary sin of Adam,
destroyed completely by the Death of Christ!
O happy fault
that earned so great, so glorious a Redeemer!
O truly blessed night,
worthy alone to know the time and hour
when Christ rose from the underworld!
This is the night
of which it is written:
The night shall be as bright as day,
dazzling is the night for me,
and full of gladness.
The sanctifying power of this night
dispels wickedness, washes faults away,
restores innocence to the fallen, and joy to mourners,
drives out hatred, fosters concord, and brings down the mighty.
On this, your night of grace, O holy Father,
accept this candle, a solemn offering,
the work of bees and of your servants' hands,
an evening sacrifice of praise,
this gift from your most holy Church.
But now we know the praises of this pillar,
which glowing fire ignites for God's honor,
a fire into many flames divided,
yet never dimmed by sharing of its light,
for it is fed by melting wax,
drawn out by mother bees
to build a torch so precious.
O truly blessed night,
when things of heaven are wed to those of earth,
and divine to the human.
Therefore, O Lord,
we pray you that this candle,
hallowed to the honor of your name,
may persevere undimmed,
to overcome the darkness of this night.
Receive it as a pleasing fragrance,
and let it mingle with the lights of heaven.
May this flame be found still burning
by the Morning Star:
the one Morning Star who never sets,
Christ your Son,
who, coming back from death's domain,
has shed his peaceful light on humanity,
and lives and reigns for ever and ever.
(*Roman Missal*, Third Typical Edition)

— 16 —

Experiencing Broken Hearts

"Father, science made my child an atheist. Now what do I do?" This question is often brought to me by someone who has a child or a friend who is gifted and brilliant with science but is struggling with their faith as well.

One of the challenges and blessings I have received as a priest is to see the perspective of both sides of this question. As the chaplain of a Catholic middle and high school, I sat with many a parent through tear-stained conversations about how they fear for their child who claims they no longer believe in God. From both my secondary education and university ministry experience, I have spoken with many youth and young adults who have claimed to be atheists, seeking me out to either explore the possibility that God may exist or to validate their newfound beliefs by attempting to provoke a combative argument with a Catholic priest. This rich tapestry of ministerial experience, combined with my love of reflecting on matters of faith and science, has helped me develop some best practices on how to address this question: How does one approach a Christian youth who has fallen away from the Church and claims to be an atheist because of science?

Principle One: Don't Mistake Confusion or Curiosity for Atheism

When someone shares with me that they have "lost their faith" and become an atheist due to science, the first question I ask is, "So you have 100 percent certainty that God does not exist and can demonstrate that to me from science?" The answer I receive to this question is telling regarding what kind of atheism I'm dealing with, if any type at all. Of the varied responses I receive, the answer is usually some variation of, "Well, no, I can't disprove God and maybe there is a God, but I know it *can't* be the Christian God."

This answer often leads to a healthy conversation which reveals that the youth really isn't an atheist but has created many perceptions about God and the Church, most of them wrong, which they simply can't accept. Whether it be evolution, the Big Bang, creationist understandings of Scripture, social issues that involve the Church, or a whole host of other issues, I find that a simple clarification of what the Church actually believes creates a moment of surprise. They are startled to learn that the things they don't believe about God are the same things I, a Catholic priest, don't believe about God. Sometimes this common "disbelief" of who God can't be can open up a healthy conversation about who God actually is.

Another answer I sometimes get is, "Father, show me where God is in the universe through the modern sciences and then I will believe God exists!" This statement usually stems from a materialist presumption that nonmaterial realities cannot exist. Therefore, God must be able to be analyzed according to some type of scientific tool. Since science does not deal with questions of God and nonmaterial realities, to ask me to prove God's existence by using science is a self-contradicting request: How can God be found through science when the very nature of science explicitly states that it isn't equipped to explore questions of God and metaphysical realities? It's a crude analogy, but to try and prove God in such a manner would be equivalent to trying to find the color red in a picture using a filter that removes all possible shades of red. You're looking for a reality that the filter used intentionally excludes. Unfortunately, this type of challenge to prove God through science usually leads to some form of, "We'll just agree to disagree."

Last, sometimes youth are just a curious lot and want to question their beliefs. From my experience, it often seems that the sophomore year of high school is the time when most students begin asking hard questions about their faith. Some of my fellow priest chaplains have called the sophomore year the "loss of soul year." Fueled in part by the normal changes all people go through at this time of life, questioning is not only a typical trait of this age group but is normal and healthy.

In addition to questioning their faith, young people also experience other transitions in their spiritual life. For example, I would often hear students in their sophomore year of high school say that the way they once prayed doesn't seem to work anymore. They also tend to question more intensely the things their parents teach them at this stage of development. The mid-teens is also the time when youth desire more independence. To summarize these traits in an accurate term that isn't always the most complimentary, they become sophomoric!

So, what is the antidote to the "loss of soul year" of high school? Simple: They eventually become juniors! Sometimes in life, you just need to walk with your child, bite your lip, and realize that you had a sophomore year in high school too — even if your rebellion looked a little different than your child's.

Principle Two: Don't Overreact, but Listen Attentively to Their Concerns

One of the biggest mistakes any of us can make in ministry or parenting is to overreact. In my first year of being a high school teacher, I had a student who was incredibly engaged with my religion class. He would seek me out after class with a list of questions, express interest in becoming a priest, and seemed to be very active in his faith. Then, one day, he just shut down and wouldn't speak to me or participate in class. I wondered if I had said something that offended him. I shared this story with a parent of another student in my class who had an exceptional faith life, asking her what I was doing wrong as a chaplain. She simply laughed and said, "Father, one thing you need to learn about kids is that they can turn on a dime and 90 percent of the time it has nothing to do with you."

Those words transformed my approach to being a chaplain and teacher. I realized that being patient and not overreacting to a student's bad day was essential to being a good teacher and a good priest. My knee-jerk responses would often lead to misunderstanding and confusion. Further, a knee-jerk overreaction to a child can create a trust barrier, as the adult's inability to stay levelheaded in the face of questions naturally makes the child pull away. In other words, never forget who the child or student is and who the parent, teacher, or pastor is when having discussions about faith and science that can irritate sensitivities.

Principle Three: Don't Underestimate the Power of Church Scandals to Impact a Young Person's Faith

From the perspective of my ministry to young people, I have come to learn a lot about the spiritual temperament of Millennials and Generation Z. For both generations, there is a built-in distrust of social superstructures, especially those that are viewed as sources of moral authority. In fact, I would argue that this distrust is growing beyond younger populations and becoming a trait of most age groups. Given the growing sentiment of distrust toward traditional sources of authority, it's not surprising that young people respond to the abuse scandals, financial corruption, or examples of incompetence in the Catholic Church's leadership and ministry by distancing themselves from the superstructure.

The moral compass for many youths is rooted primarily in relationships, such as those with friends, family, teachers, and their local priest. The Church can be a part of their moral compass, but it is more from the disposition of "I know and trust *my* priest, so I trust what *he* says about God" while they simultaneously maintain a suspicious attitude toward the Catholic Church as a whole. Therefore, we are entering a cultural era of post-establishment thinking in which relationship drives faith decisions more than tradition and authority. In many ways, I think there is a way to see a subtle good in this shift. As Catholics, we need to strive to live what we proclaim and not simply think that knowledge of faith is sufficient.

Principle Four: The Ultimate Goal Is to Make the Discussion about Faith and Science

A thread that I hope is self-evident through the previous principles is that most of the obstacles to having a healthy conversation about faith and science have very little to do with the perceived tension between the two. Instead, epic fights between faith and science are often a smoke screen for deeper hurts and wounds, and for the distrust that people have toward the Church — and these have little to do with Darwin and Stephen Hawking.

In fact, I find that the more emotional someone is with me when voicing their views on faith and science, the more likely the true issue has nothing to do with faith and science. Perhaps it was a priest that was dismissive of them in their youth and, in that hurt, they turned away from God. Perhaps they found their parents' faith to be overbearing and yearned to be free from the weight of feeling forced into a religion they have legitimate questions about. These types of wounds can create a mentality of, "I can't trust the Church because of this experience; therefore, I will question everything the Church stands for (or I *think* she stands for)!"

Scripture

The fifteenth chapter of the Gospel of Luke provides us with a powerful string of reconciliation parables: The Lost Sheep, The Lost Coin, and The Prodigal Son. These are passages that come to mind when I think of people I love and minister to who have turned away from the Catholic Faith. I would encourage you to pray with all the parables if you know someone in your life who has drifted from their faith, or if you find yourself feeling lost in your relationship with God. I have provided the most famous of these parables below with the story of the Prodigal Son, but I also wanted to offer some excerpts for reflection from the other passages too. When we understand these parables properly, the real narrative is that none of us is really lost, but we are all wounded and in need of love. Pray that God pours out his love on you today so that you may rediscover the joy of being home.

15:4–7 (The Lost Sheep)

"What man among you having a hundred sheep and losing one of them would not leave the ninety-nine in the desert and go after the lost one until he finds it? And when he does find it, he sets it on his shoulders with great joy and, upon his arrival home, he calls together his friends and neighbors and says to them, 'Rejoice with me because I have found my lost sheep.' I tell you, in just the same way there will be more joy in heaven over one sinner who repents than over ninety-nine righteous people who have no need of repentance."

15:8–10 (The Lost Coin)

"Or what woman having ten coins and losing one would not light a lamp and sweep the house, searching carefully until she finds it? And when she does find it, she calls together her friends and neighbors and says to them, 'Rejoice with me because I have found the coin that I lost.' In just the same way, I tell you, there will be rejoicing among the angels of God over one sinner who repents."

15:11–32 (The Parable of the Lost Son)

Then he said, "A man had two sons, and the younger son said to his father, 'Father, give me the share of your estate that should come to me.' So the father divided the property between them.

After a few days, the younger son collected all his belongings and set off to a distant country where he squandered his inheritance on a life of dissipation. When he had freely spent everything, a severe famine struck that country, and he found himself in dire need. So he hired himself out to one of the local citizens who sent him to his farm to tend the swine. And he longed to eat his fill of the pods on which the swine fed, but nobody gave him any.

Coming to his senses he thought, 'How many of my father's hired workers have more than enough food to eat, but here am I, dying from hunger. I shall get up and go to my father and I shall say to him, "Father, I have sinned against heaven and against you. I no longer deserve to be called your son; treat me as you would treat one of your hired workers."'

So he got up and went back to his father.

While he was still a long way off, his father caught sight of him, and was filled with compassion. He ran to his son, embraced him and kissed him. His son said to him, 'Father, I have sinned against heaven and against you; I no longer deserve to be called your son.'

But his father ordered his servants, 'Quickly bring the finest robe and put it on him; put a ring on his finger and sandals on his feet. Take the fattened calf and slaughter it. Then let us celebrate with a feast, because this son of mine was dead, and has come to life again; he was lost, and has been found.' Then the celebration began.

Now the older son had been out in the field and, on his way back, as he neared the house, he heard the sound of music and dancing. He called one of the servants and asked what this might mean. The servant said to him, 'Your brother has returned and your father has slaughtered the fattened calf because he has him back safe and sound.'

He became angry, and when he refused to enter the house, his father came out and pleaded with him. He said to his father in reply, 'Look, all these years I served you and not once did I disobey your orders; yet you never gave me even a young goat to feast on with my friends. But when your son returns who swallowed up your property with prostitutes, for him you slaughter the fattened calf.'

He said to him, 'My son, you are here with me always; everything I have is yours. But now we must celebrate and rejoice, because your brother was dead and has come to life again; he was lost and has been found.'"

I can't even begin to imagine the deep wounds that have been brought to light with the priest abuse scandal. What impact does clergy sexual abuse or sexual abuse by anyone in the Church have upon a survivor's faith? When I pray about these scandals, I am often deeply moved by the thought, "How deep must their faith be to continue to walk through the door of the Church in light of what they have suffered!"

Amid this sea of hurt and distrust, I often find that the first step is *not* to talk about whether the Higgs boson particle should be named the "God particle," but to focus on the healing the person really needs. These wounds can run deep, so deep that reentering the Church on their own may not be possible for them, at least at this point in their life. Yet, it is this reality that makes me appreciate more deeply Pope Francis's call for spiritual accompaniment, for walking with one another in the Lord. After fifteen years of priesthood, I have come to learn that dealing with questions of faith and science is quite easy — presuming that is what the question is actually about. Walking with people through the pain of, "This is how I feel hurt and abandoned by God and the Church" is a completely different journey, requiring different "best practices" I will be working on for the rest of my priesthood.

Spiritual Exercise

Do you have a "lost sheep" in your life who is struggling with his or her faith? Perhaps you are reading this because you feel a bit lost in your own faith life. Regardless of where one may be in their faith journey, more often than not I find that leaving the Christian faith often has less to do with honest questions of faith and science and more to do with hurt, woundedness, or a feeling of abandonment.

Do you struggle with questions of faith and science, or is your heart at peace with this relationship? Are there deep hurts and wounds that you wrestle with, making trust in God and those who minister in God's name rather difficult? Do you know someone who is in desperate need of spiritual accompaniment, yearning for someone who will share their faith with them and walk with them to help them find healing from God? Pray with these questions. Let us walk with each other in faith. And let us pray that someday the biggest problem the Church will face will simply be honest questions about faith and science instead of the sea of wounds and hurts that often fuel distrust in the Church.

— 17 —

Do Faith, Do Science

When our workshops began, I had a preconceived notion of what the answers to questions of faith and science would be. As is often the case, the journey on which ACME has taken me has revealed a very different end point. I falsely presumed that I would find clear, air-tight answers that would ultimately declare a victor and a loser. I should have known better. What God led me to through our workshops is a deepening of my understanding of the relationship between faith and reason. I didn't encounter a duelistic volatility of people of faith duking it out with people of science. Instead, I found myself on a journey, a pilgrimage of the mind and heart that deepened my love of him who is the author of both the Book of Nature and the Book of Scripture. I found peace between faith and science, not war.

Part of that peace emanates from the fact that both faith and science are part of the human experience. They are not dueling quasi-deities locked in an eternal battle. Faith and science are things people do and embrace to help make sense of our world, to help us find solutions during struggles, and to help us find joy, wonder, and meaning.

Faith and science help us delve into some of the larger questions of life by looking at how we got here and what our purpose for existing is. Yes, faith explores the "why" questions and science deals primarily with the "how" questions, but both are needed to help us understand the human experience. Trying to pit the two against each other is one of the most basic errors we can make. In fact, the seed of this "both/and" approach to faith and science was addressed by Saint Augustine far before the advent of modern science. Here is a profound insight from his work, *On the Literal Interpretation of Genesis*:

> Usually, even a non-Christian knows something about the earth, the heavens, and the other elements of this world, about the motion and orbit of the stars and even their size and relative positions, about the predictable eclipses of the sun and

> moon, the cycles of the years and the seasons, about the kinds of animals, shrubs, stones, and so forth, and this knowledge he holds to as being certain from reason and experience.
>
> Now, it is a disgraceful and dangerous thing for [a nonbeliever] to hear a Christian, presumably giving the meaning of Holy Scripture, talking nonsense on these topics; and we should take all means to prevent such an embarrassing situation, in which people show up vast ignorance in a Christian and laugh it to scorn. The shame is not so much that an ignorant individual is derided, but that people outside the household of faith think our sacred writers held such opinions, and, to the great loss of those for whose salvation we toil, the writers of our Scripture are criticized and rejected as unlearned men.

Saint Augustine's reflection reminds us that at its heart, Catholicism is the exploration of truth through faith *and* reason. The Book of Scripture and the Book of Nature are complementary. Pope Benedict XVI explained in a 2008 address to the Pontifical Council of Sciences that both books, Scripture and Nature, find their same origin in God's creative act. Benedict further explained that for science, philosophy, and theology to explore our created world, there first needs to be a universe of wonder to explore:

> To "evolve" literally means "to unroll a scroll," that is, to read a book. The imagery of nature as a book has its roots in Christianity and has been held dear by many scientists. Galileo saw nature as a book whose author is God in the same way that Scripture has God as its author. It is a book whose history, whose evolution, whose "writing" and meaning, we "read" according to the different approaches of the sciences, while all the time presupposing the foundational presence of the author who has wished to reveal himself therein. This image also helps us to understand that the world, far from originating out of chaos, resembles an ordered book; it is a cosmos. Notwithstanding elements of the irrational, chaotic and the destructive in the long processes of change in the cosmos, matter as such is "legible." It has an inbuilt "mathematics." The human mind therefore can engage not only in a "cosmography" studying measurable phenomena but also in a "cosmology" discerning the visible inner logic of the cosmos. We may not at first be able to see the harmony both of the whole and of the relations of the individual parts, or their relationship to the whole. Yet, there always remains a broad range of intelligible events, and the process is rational in that it reveals an order of evident correspondences and undeniable finalities: in the inorganic world, between microstructure and macrostructure; in the organic and animal world, between structure and function; and in the spiritual world, between knowledge of the truth and the aspiration to freedom.

As created beings in this creation of wonder, we find a dynamic, changing, and evolving cosmos that is deep and mysterious. Some in our day see evolution as something that is

Spiritual Exercise and Scripture

Below is one of the most beautiful hymns of praise we find in the Bible. As the Prophet Daniel speaks of all creation praising God, I invite you to add your voice to this great hymn.

Bless the Lord, all you works of the Lord,
praise and exalt him above all forever.
Angels of the Lord, bless the Lord,
praise and exalt him above all forever.
You heavens, bless the Lord,
praise and exalt him above all forever.
All you waters above the heavens, bless the Lord,
praise and exalt him above all forever.
All you powers, bless the Lord;
praise and exalt him above all forever.
Sun and moon, bless the Lord;
praise and exalt him above all forever.
Stars of heaven, bless the Lord;
praise and exalt him above all forever.
Every shower and dew, bless the Lord;
praise and exalt him above all forever.
All you winds, bless the Lord;
praise and exalt him above all forever.
Fire and heat, bless the Lord;
praise and exalt him above all forever.
Cold and chill, bless the Lord;
praise and exalt him above all forever.
Dew and rain, bless the Lord;
praise and exalt him above all forever.
Frost and chill, bless the Lord;
praise and exalt him above all forever.
Hoarfrost and snow, bless the Lord;
praise and exalt him above all forever.
Nights and days, bless the Lord;
praise and exalt him above all forever.
Light and darkness, bless the Lord;
praise and exalt him above all forever.
Lightnings and clouds, bless the Lord;
praise and exalt him above all forever.
Let the earth bless the Lord,
praise and exalt him above all forever.
Mountains and hills, bless the Lord;
praise and exalt him above all forever.
Everything growing on earth, bless the Lord;
praise and exalt him above all forever.
You springs, bless the Lord;
praise and exalt him above all forever.
Seas and rivers, bless the Lord;
praise and exalt him above all forever.
You sea monsters and all water creatures, bless the Lord;
praise and exalt him above all forever.
All you birds of the air, bless the Lord;
praise and exalt him above all forever.
All you beasts, wild and tame, bless the Lord;
praise and exalt him above all forever.
All you mortals, bless the Lord;
praise and exalt him above all forever.
O Israel, bless the Lord;
praise and exalt him above all forever.
Priests of the Lord, bless the Lord;
praise and exalt him above all forever.
Servants of the Lord, bless the Lord;
praise and exalt him above all forever.
Spirits and souls of the just, bless the Lord;
praise and exalt him above all forever.
Holy and humble of heart, bless the Lord;
praise and exalt him above all forever.
Hananiah, Azariah, Mishael, bless the Lord;
praise and exalt him above all forever.

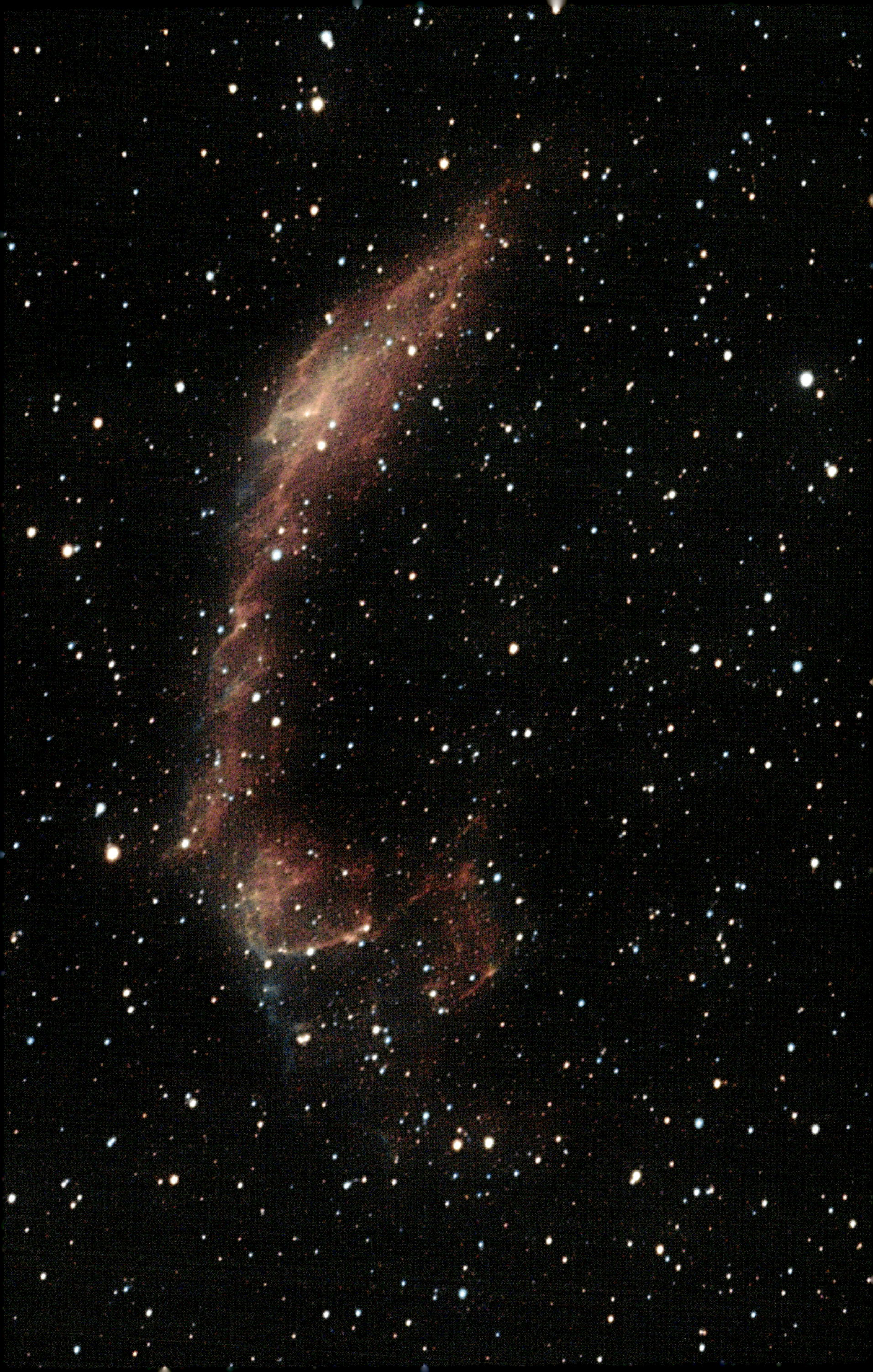

against faith, yet Benedict reminds us that *to evolve* means "to unroll as a scroll," making the study of evolution a necessary part of reading the Book of Nature.

Part of the confusion around evolution derives from conflating the observational science of how things change over time with the philosophical Darwinism that takes those observations and makes erroneous claims that they prove that the changes in nature occur without God. The Church rightly rejects the Darwinian denial of God but is very open to the possibility that the physical "stuff" we are made of came from other creatures. While still a cardinal, Benedict offered a clear explanation of the relationship between faith and evolution in one of his homilies on creation:

> We cannot say: creation or evolution, inasmuch as these two things respond to two different realities. The story of the dust of the earth and the breath of God … does not in fact explain how human persons come to be but rather what they are. It explains their inmost origin and casts light on the project that they are. And, vice versa, the theory of evolution seeks to understand and describe biological

> developments. But in so doing it cannot explain where the "project" of human persons comes from, nor their inner origin, nor their particular nature. To that extent we are faced here with two complementary — rather than mutually exclusive — realities. ('*In the Beginning ...*')

This reflection by Benedict should not be a surprise for Catholics. Going back to Pius XII we see a growing series of papal statements finding a peaceful relationship between Christian faith and evolution. In 2007, Benedict reiterated his thoughts from before his papal election during a question and answer with clergy on retreat:

> Currently, I see in Germany, but also in the United States, a somewhat fierce debate raging between so-called creationism and evolutionism, presented as though they were mutually exclusive alternatives: those who believe in the Creator would not be able to conceive of evolution, and those who instead support evolution would have to exclude God. This antithesis is absurd because, on the one hand, there are so many scientific proofs in favor of evolution which appears to be a reality we can see and which enriches our knowledge of life and being as such.

Getting the question of evolution right as people of faith is so important. If we continue down the path of attacking evolution, the rift between people of faith and people of science will only deepen. Instead, let us embrace the places where we can agree about our material origins, while also being clear that those material realities do not and cannot make any theological statements about God. True science stays neutral on the questions of God. It is not equipped to make assertions about theological matters.

Another aspect of approaching the Books of Scripture and Nature is not only to study faith and science but to *do* faith and science. For both people of faith and science, there has never been a better time to pursue both! Social media has bountiful resources to grow in our prayer life, to learn and participate in the sciences, and to find practical opportunities to incorporate science into our faith life. The key is to make sure the sources perused are credible and healthy. I highly recommend the Vatican Observatory's webpage and blog, *Sacred Space Astronomy*. There are numerous citizen science programs you can find on professional astronomy — resources like NASA, the European Space Agency, and "porthole" websites like Zooniverse. My one suggestion is that when approaching these resources, make sure they are doing real science and providing spiritual resources for authentic faith. For every good resource, there is a plethora of propaganda resources as well. In short, be discerning in choosing faith and science resources to embrace.

All of us, even those of us who are not professional scientists, can do science in small ways. And doing science in small ways, while continuing to practice our faith, gives us a deeper appreciation of how faith and science relate to one another.

I would also encourage you not only to explore questions through cyberspace, but to interact in positive, charitable ways with people of faith and science. Remember Dr. Leonard from earlier in this book, who discovered a comet that now bears his name? While he was showing us some simple examples of how comparing a series of images helped him find Comet Leonard, it reminded me of doing similar image comparisons for a citizen science project on Zooniverse. When I shared this with Dr. Leonard, he was excited to share that his observatory hosts some Zooniverse projects. It was a moment where doing science wasn't just about staring at computer screens, but realizing that there are real people behind these projects. And when we meet these people, the passion to help their research continues.

This emphasis on real human contact as part of doing real science should also be at the heart of approaching the night sky with our faith. There are very good online resources we can access to learn about faith and the night sky, and many people I know have some type of cellphone app that provides them with a real-time star chart to help them find constellations. Always remember that these resources which assist are precisely that: an aid. Just as Christians know that there is a difference between reading the Bible as a book of literature and praying with the Bible as divinely inspired text, so,

too, is there a big difference between learning about the night sky and encountering the night sky. Whether it be the covenant with Abraham, God's discourse with Job, the hymns of creation in the psalms, or the celestial implication of the re-creation Christ promises in the Book of Revelation, the night sky is part of our spiritual language. God invites us to have a playful relationship with the signs, symbols, and metaphors in the stars.

Yes, the end points of questions of faith and science are not always what we presume them to be. The true end point of a dialogue between faith and science is awe and wonder, the gift of the Holy Spirit we call fear of the Lord. And since Scripture states that fear of the Lord is the beginning of wisdom (see Prv 9:10), we do not arrive at an ending cadence, but at a starting point. It is, as Saint Bonaventure presents to us, the first step in our spiritual ascent. It is the beginning of our understanding and embracing of the God who created us. It is our maiden voyage to a life of faith, hope, and love.

Appendix

Ode to a Spiritual and Intellectual Father

As you have explored these reflections on the night sky, you have probably noticed that there are many references to Pope Benedict XVI. While I was in seminary, Joseph Cardinal Ratzinger was on just about every reading list for my classes. I am not an expert on his writing by any stretch of the imagination. Still, I consider him to be a kind of spiritual and intellectual father to me. I love his clear, systematic thinking and how he had the ability to surprise those who came to assumptions about him.

I wrote a series of reflections on Benedict XVI's collection of homilies on creation just before he passed away. As an ode to Pope Benedict, I wish to share those reflections to honor him who greatly shaped my thinking on faith and science through his own reflections on God and the study of our world.

Reflection on the First Homily from *'In the Beginning ...'*

What do you remember about Pope Benedict XVI? It wouldn't surprise me if much of your memory is about his administrative roles and his historic resignation. As Prefect of the Dicastery for the Doctrine of the Faith, Cardinal joseph Ratzinger was known as a "theological conservative," earning him the nickname "God's Rottweiler."

When he was elected Pope Benedict XVI, some were surprised that he started to write about things like care for creation — a "theologically progressive" topic. Benedict's nickname soon switched from "God's Rottweiler" to "God's German Shepherd" and "the Green Pope." What was the change in Benedict's theological approach?

The irony is that there wasn't a change. Having read much of Benedict's early writings in seminary, it was evident to me that his thought transcended typical "traditional and progressive" labels. Instead, his thought was an ongoing commentary on what it means to think and act in an unapologetically and faithfully Catholic manner.

Part of that unapologetic approach was about the relationship between faith and science. A very good starting point to understand his thinking on the subject can be found in a collection of four homilies titled *'In the Beginning ...' A Catholic Understanding of the Story of Creation and the Fall.* This collection was done before he was elected pope and was still Joseph Cardinal Ratzinger.

In the first homily of this collection, Ratzinger points out a clear question that cuts to the heart of the tension between faith and science: How do we reconcile our understanding of modern science with the biblical narrative of creation?

After presenting some of the modern missteps regarding the slow rejection of Genesis in favor of the modern sciences, Ratzinger lays out some basic distinctions between Scripture and science. The first, and one of the most foundational considerations in properly understanding a healthy relationship between faith and science, is that the Bible is not a scientific text and should not be treated as such.

To clarify this distinction, Ratzinger explains the difference between the *form* of the portrayal of creation in Scripture and the *content* of what is portrayed:

> The form would have been chosen from what was understandable at the time — from the images which surrounded the people who lived then, which they used in speaking and in thinking, and thanks to which they were able to understand the greater realities. And only the reality that shines through these images would be what was intended and what was truly enduring. Thus Scripture would not wish to inform us about how the different species of plant life gradually appeared or how the sun and the moon and the stars were established. Its purpose ultimately would be to say one thing: God created the world.

This beautiful distinction between form and content does raise a question: Does this mean that Genesis is "just another creation story" that can't speak to our modern situation? Ratzinger beautifully explains that the true "history" of Scripture is not defined in the categories of who, what, when, where, and how, but is a history of God's struggle with us to make himself known, and our struggle to embrace and know the God who seeks us.

From this standpoint, the creation narrative is truly one of ongoing creation as God journeys with the children of Israel in the Old Testament and guides, through the Holy Spirit, the development of the infant Church in the New Testament. God "recreates this world" time and time again, whether it be the waters of the Red Sea or the waters of baptism, to accomplish one simple goal: *an encounter with God in love.*

Ratzinger then explains how other ancient religions would have appeared to have had much more power and prestige in the worldly sense. The gods of the mystery religions pointed to violence and evil, and formed warring factions that came into the world through violence and tried to set the world right through violence. The scriptural account, on the other hand, presents a different starting point: *The earth was without form and void* (see Gn 1:2).

Absent in these words are the sinister, brutal, and violent activities of warring gods of sun, moon, water, wind, fire, rain, and so forth. Instead, Ratzinger presents an image of biblical creation that seems much more domestic than epic:

> When the sun and the moon are referred to as lamps that God has hung in the sky for the measurement of time, to the people of that age it must have seemed a terrible sacrilege to designate the great gods sun and moon as lamps for measuring time. Here we see the audacity and the temperateness of the faith that, in confronting the pagan myths, made the light of truth appear by showing that the world was not a demonic contest but that it arose from God's Reason and reposes on God's Word.

The hope of the children of Israel was not to be rooted in violence, power, and war, but in truth, reason, and the peace that came from knowing that no matter where they traveled, no matter where they rested, they were living in and a part of God's creation.

The homily concludes with how the Law and Prophets point us to the promised *Word*, Jesus Christ. The use of *Logos* or Word by Ratzinger is intentional to point out that Christian faith is reasonable, creation is reasonable, and that it is reasonable to embrace a Creator whose reasonableness is on full display through our scientific exploration of creation.

There is more but this will suffice to invite you to reflect on the following questions: What is your "beginning"? Is God your "Beginning"? If so, how is that Beginning seeking to recreate you this day?

Reflection on the Second Homily

When we explore the second homily in the collected homilies of Joseph Cardinal Ratzinger, we encounter a reflection on Genesis 1:20–24. The future pope begins with a beautiful summary of two core realizations about the creation narratives and the Church's authentic understanding of them:

First, biblical literalism is not the proper reading of creation, and second, the reasonableness of creation points to embracing both the "that" of creation (scientific exploration) and the "why" of creation (philosophical and theological exploration into the meaning of creation).

In the next section of the homily, Ratzinger provides a brief history of scientific cosmology. He reflects on the scientific presumption of an eternal cosmos that was later questioned by the law of entropy. From there he reflects on the development of the Theory of Relativity and a growing sentiment that creation itself is reasonable, pointing to what I am calling a "Reasoner": "In what is most vast, in the world of heavenly bodies, we see revealed a powerful Reason that holds the universe together. And we are penetrating ever deeper into what is smallest, into the cell and into the primordial units of life; here, too, we discover a Reason that astounds us."

What I find so refreshing about Ratzinger's reflection on the reasonableness of creation is that it invites us not to fear the scientific method, liberating the Christian from the burden of trying to "disprove" theories of which we have little to no understanding.

Ratzinger's thought reminds me of a brilliant insight given by Fr. Gabor, SJ at the first Faith and Astronomy Workshop (now Astronomy for Catholics in Ministry and Education), where he stated that the self-evident intelligibility of creation can easily make us forget that there is nothing in faith or science that necessitates that the created world be intelligible. The universe could just as easily have been inaccessible to our ability to reason. It is as if the universe wants to be known or that something wants to be known through the universe.

When I share these reflections with Christians, I receive a wide range of responses. Some of my friends who wish to have a more literalist approach to Scripture presume that I (and Pope Benedict) am rejecting biblical faith by being open to science and by not seeing science as contradicting Genesis.

What surprises me and concerns me even more is when good Catholics whose faith I deeply respect think that I reject Catholic teaching on creation. Quite to the contrary, I am deeply invested in understanding the "literal sense" of Scripture as a Catholic, but the literal sense and literalism are two profoundly different approaches to Scripture.

The authentic math of the Bible, Ratzinger writes, points us to the true high point of creation — the timeless day, the call to Sabbath, the call to worship: "Creation is oriented to the sabbath, which is the sign of the covenant between God and humankind. In a short while we shall have to reflect more closely on this, but for the time being, as a first step, we can draw this conclusion: Creation is designed in such a way that it is oriented to worship."

Something I think would be good for all of us to reflect upon is the question: How do we view the Sabbath in our own lives? Do we see it as a reminder of God's covenant of love for us or do we simply make it another day in our week? May we not only keep holy the Sabbath but also allow God's covenant of love to dwell deep within our hearts and be expressed in our thoughts and actions.

Reflection on the Third Homily

In his third homily, the future pope explores one of the most fundamental questions as it pertains to you and me: What is a human and what does it mean to be human?

Two "simple" questions, right? Yet, as with many simple questions, the exploration of their answers leads us down paths of insight that are not foreseen.

To get our bearings on the distinction between what a human is and what it means to be human, I'd like to draw from the wisdom of one of my former seminary professors, Dr. David Fagerberg. When I was a part of Dr. Fagerberg's sacramental theology course, he made a distinction for us between two ways of viewing a sacrament: the Patristic approach (which studies the Christian writers from the earliest days of the Church) and the later Scholastic approach to sacramental thought. To clarify this distinction, he used the analogy of how we can study the existence of a frog in a science lab. One way is to study how a living frog moves, behaves, interacts with, and impacts the world around it. The other way is to dissect the frog and study its "outers" and "innards."

Dr. Fagerberg explained that the sacramental mind of the Patristics focuses primarily on "how the frog hops," being preoccupied with how sacramental grace moves us, impacts us, and transforms us. The Scholastic sacramental mind is drawn to "frog dissection," primarily interested in how we understand what a sacrament is from the standpoint of matter, form, substance, and essence. This distinction is not absolute; both the Patristic and Scholastic schools of thought explore the *"what is it"* and *"how does it"* aspects of sacramental thought. However, Dr. Fagerberg used this analogy to draw attention to the emphasis of each school of thought.

This serves as a good backdrop to explore Ratzinger's thought on the human person in light of Genesis. The first insight gleaned from the Book of Genesis on what a person "is" is simple and straightforward to Ratzinger: We are dirt. As uninspiring as that may seem on the surface, there is deep theological significance to this observation. The first creation narrative speaks of the goodness of creation and how, when God looked upon all of creation, it was "good good" (to offer a more literal English translation of the Hebrew). To say that the human person is dirt is not a derogatory or disrespectful statement, but it reminds us that we are made of the same substance as all of creation. We are "good stuff"!

The fact that we are all dirt — or to quote the Committal Rite of the Church, "We are dust and to dust we shall return" — is also a unifying aspect of the human person. We are not only taken from the Earth, but we are also taken from this *one* Earth. Therefore, we are to strive to see every person as having equal dignity regardless of race, creed, gender, state of life, or country of origin. To deny this truth, Ratzinger writes, is to drift into the many false teachings of history in regard to the human person.

This first insight is one that I think can be universally understood regardless of one's faith. The next insight transitions into the more philosophical and theological aspects of understanding humanity: The human person is made in God's image and likeness.

In Ratzinger's eyes, being uniquely made in God's image and likeness is intimately tied to God's desire to be in a unique relationship of love with us:

> In the human being heaven and earth touch one another. In the human being God enters into his creation; the human being is directly related to God. The human being is called by him. … Each human being is known by God and loved by him. Each is willed by God, and each is God's image. Precisely in this consists the deeper and greater unity of humankind — that each of us, each individual human being, realizes the one project of God and has his or her origin in the same creative idea of God.

Of the many attempts I have heard over the years to present a starting point for explaining the "image and likeness of God," I seldom have encountered such beautifully simple and clear ideas:

- First — The breath of God and the dirt we are made of is a meeting point between heaven and Earth.
- Second — We are called, known, named, claimed, and loved.
- Third — We are God's desire, and God has placed desire in us as part of his plan of salvation.
- Fourth — To hurt another person is to hurt both God and what belongs to God.
- Fifth — We bear God's image because God actively seeks to be in relationship with us.

Now, somewhere in that list, I think we're seeing the transition from "frog dissection" to "the hopping frog" — the distinction between what a human being is and what it means to be a human being. It is one thing to reflect upon what constitutes the substance of our existence (dirt). It's another question to reflect upon the substance of our lives (loving and being loved, desiring and being desirable, knowing and being known, etc.).

I invite you to take the following questions to prayer to explore your own understanding of what you are and who you are:

- Do you see yourself as a meeting point between heaven and Earth?
- Are you aware that God calls, knows, names, claims, and loves you?
- How does it impact you to know that you are desired by God and that the desire you have is a gift from God?
- When hurt arises, do you see that hurt as something that also offends God?
- What are the key relationships in your life, including those with the people close to you and God, that bring joy and love to your heart?

Pray with these questions. Give thanks to God that you are dirt! Give thanks that you are a part of this good Earth. And give thanks that God has chosen you to be a meeting point between heaven and Earth.

Requiescat in Pace Benedict XVI

My last reflection on Benedict's homilies came at the time of his death. This development made my final reflection less about the fourth homily on creation and more about offering a broader *In Memoriam* to Benedict.

What is the legacy of Pope Benedict XVI? For some, a legacy becomes a litany of what a person has accomplished in life. From this perspective, we can explore Benedict XVI's legacy as a dry listing of significant dates in his life, positions held in the Church, professional feuds, his numerous publications, and so forth. All of these details would fit nicely into the theme of, "This is what Pope Benedict did."

However, we can also explore a legacy from the standpoint of who a person is at their core. This approach can be a bit more challenging because it presumes an inner understanding of a person that is, in many ways, deeper than the person's awareness of themselves. If the goal of understanding a legacy is to know the depths of another's inner being, we must understand that only God, to steal from Saint Augustine, possesses the depths of someone's legacy.

This distinction is fitting when trying to understand the inner heart of Benedict XVI. He was deeply Augustinian in his thinking and emphasized a profound, personal encounter with God as the starting point of his theology. This starting point is strongly emphasized in his first encyclical, *Deus Caritas Est*: "Being Christian is not the result of an ethical choice or a lofty idea, but the encounter with an event, a person, which gives life a new horizon and a decisive direction."

This sentiment of having intense closeness to God who is, in turn, intensely close to creation informed his closing thoughts in this collection of homilies. In conclusion, he offered a strong critique of modernism's attempts to remove the Church's Doctrine of Creation from the cultural discussion of the natural world.

Ironically, Benedict's first critique of the modernist move was to point out the error of Giordano Bruno's "divine cosmos." No, it wasn't Bruno's understanding of heliocentrism that Benedict found problematic, but his desire to recapitulate Greek polytheism, which sees the whole of creation as an already harmonious nexus of divinized relations at peace with themselves. This thought of Bruno is in direct contrast to the Christian understanding of a Creator whose creation has fallen.

This fallen world is a nexus of natural limitations and contingent relationships — a world that isn't a pluralism of gods but consists of form and substance brought into existence by the Creator. This world of limits stands as an obstacle, for Bruno, to true freedom. To him, "the dependence implied by faith in creation is unacceptable. It is seen as the real barrier to human freedom, the basis of all other restrictions, the first thing needing to be eliminated if humankind is to be effectively liberated." (*'In the Beginning ...'*, 84)

Benedict's second critique sees the move away from the Doctrine of Creation in the modern world as a byproduct of Galileo. Again, not questioning Galileo's heliocentrism, Benedict argues that as Galileo rose in influence, the Book of Nature started to be reduced to a mathematical exploration of creation. This shift, Benedict asserts, turned creation into an object of study divorced from the broader sense of the concept of creation. This turn eventually bled into theology, slowly changing our view of a God with whom we have a dynamic relationship to an abstract and distant "it":

> [God] dwindles away to be little more than the formal mathematical structures perceived by science in nature. ... A mere "first cause," which is effective only in nature and never reveals itself to humans, which abandons humans — has to

> abandon them — to a realm completely beyond its own sphere of influence, such a first cause is no longer God but a scientific hypothesis. On the other hand, a God who has nothing to do with the rationality of creation, but is effective only in the inner world of piety, is also no longer God; he becomes devoid of reality and ultimately meaningless. Only when creation and covenant come together can either creation or covenant be realistically discussed — the one presupposes the other. (*'In the Beginning ...'*, 85)

In short, we begin to see a creeping philosophy which distances God from our understanding of the created world. This distancing transforms God from someone with whom we have a dynamic relationship to more of a deistic version of a god akin to the thought of Spinoza: God may have started it all but now stands in the back and is distant from all of us.

The more modernity seeks to redefine freedom in individualistic terms and relegate God to a distant "it," the less we emphasize not only a dynamic relationship with God, but also a dynamic relationship with God's creation and how we are to care for this gift.

There is much more that should be said of Benedict XVI's thought on faith and science, which is why he will be read for generations to come. To conclude this reflection on Pope Benedict but also to tie together the themes in this book, I ask you to reflect on these questions in prayer:

- Is your relationship with God a dynamic and life-giving relationship or has God become a distant "it" in your life?
- Are you willing to see in our created world a dynamic creation that bears the fingerprints of the Creator whose presence we can't escape, or do you tend to see the world as just a "thing" that we use and move through with little meaning or purpose?

My hope and prayer is that these reflections have provided for you new eyes and a new approach to see God through the beauty of the night sky, the created world around us, through each other, and through the modes of Christ's presence offered to us in Word and Sacrament. Let us not allow the world to bully God out of our cultural consciousness or to reduce our world to a drab and monochrome "thing." Instead, let us allow the vibrance of God's love and our embrace of that love to breathe new color and vibrance into our world.

In this time when many are consumed by darkness, may the light shining in the darkness, Jesus Christ, guide us, awaken us, and renew us in love.

Acknowledgments

I would like to thank Michael Brown for donating many of his images of the night sky for this book. Also, I would like to thank OSV for the opportunity to share this journey with you.

Artwork

Pages 12–13: Panoramic view of the Milky Way, taken from the Kurzynski family farm (the author's childhood home).

Page 14: Stars in the Milky Way Galaxy with the core (or center) of our celestial home over the horizon. The streak of light is a small meteor burning up in the atmosphere. Photo taken at a small lake just north of New Auburn, Wisconsin.

Page 18: Night scene from Big Falls Park in Eau Claire, Wisconsin.

Page 21: The larger of the two objects is the Whirlpool Galaxy and the small object is a smaller dwarf galaxy. The two objects interact with each other and are 24 to 30 million light years away from Earth. Both galaxies are observable with good binoculars, but to the naked eye they appear small and fuzzy. These types of images are possible only with long exposure astrophotography through a telescope. Photo taken by Mike Brown of the Chippewa Valley Astronomical Society. Used with permission.

Page 24: Heart Nebula (IC 1805). Nebulae are dust clouds, and the pink color of the cloud means the dust and gases are hot enough to emit their own light (emission nebulae). Some emission nebulae are where infant stars are born. These dust clouds are about 7,500 light years away from Earth. Photo taken by Mike Brown of the Chippewa Valley Astronomical Society. Used with permission.

Page 27: Spider and Fly Nebulae (IC 417 and NGC 1931). These dust clouds are about 7,500 light years away from Earth. Photo taken by Mike Brown of the Chippewa Valley Astronomical Society. Used with permission.

Page 28: Horsehead Nebula (B 33). Have you ever looked at the belt of Orion? Right under the first star of the belt is a combination of different kinds of space dust. The Horsehead Nebula is a dark nebula, meaning the dust and gas in this cloud are not hot enough to emit their own light, and there isn't a star close enough for the object to reflect its light. It is 1,500 light years away from Earth. This image was taken by the staff at the Vatican Observatory using an Advanced Technology Telescope (VATT).

Page 33: The Pleiades Cluster, also known as the "Seven Sisters." Observable with the naked eye or through a pair of low-powered binoculars, this stunning open cluster of stars is only 444 light years away from Earth. The blue dust clouds (reflection nebula, meaning the dust and gas of the cloud are not hot enough to emit their own light, but a bright neighboring star illuminates the clouds) surrounding the stars are not visible to the naked eye. Photo taken by Mike Brown of the Chippewa Valley Astronomical Society. Used with permission.

Page 34: The Ghost of Cassiopia (IC 63). This faint nebula is found in the constellation Cassiopia, and its shape resembles a ghost. This nebula is about 550 light years away from Earth.

Pages 38–39: A meteor streaks across the sky during the annual Perseid meteor shower on August 11, 2021, in Spruce Knob, West Virginia. Science History Images / Alamy Stock Photo.

Page 41: Jellyfish Nebula (IC 443). This emission nebula, approximately 5,000 light years away from Earth, was formed by a star that went supernova more than 30,000 years ago. A supernova occurs when a star that is at least five times larger than our sun collapses in on itself and then blows its outer layers into space. Depending on the collapse, supernovae can create black holes or neutron stars. It is believed that the Jellyfish Nebula is a remnant from a neighboring neutron star. Supernovae also create heavier elements that "seed" planets with elements not present on their surface. It is thought that elements needed for the human person to exist came from these supernovae. Photo taken by Mike Brown of the Chippewa Valley Astronomical Society. Used with permission.

Pages 44–45: Comet Neowise over downtown Eau Claire, Wisconsin.

Page 48: The Flaming Star Nebula (IC 405). This nebula is about 1,500 light years away from Earth. Photo taken by Mike Brown of the Chippewa Valley Astronomical Society. Used with permission.

Page 52: Andromeda Galaxy. Did you ever play "chicken" as a child? You know, the game where you would run right at a friend and see which one would jump out of the way first? Andromeda and the Milky Way Galaxy are in a type of intergalactic chicken game. Both galaxies are moving toward each other and will run into each other in about 4.5 billion years (so you don't need to lose any sleep about this chicken match. We will most likely see this, God willing, from the perspective of eternity). Photo taken by Mike Brown of the Chippewa Valley Astronomical Society. Used with permission.

Page 55: Rho Ophiuchi Cloud Complex. This complex object, approximately 460 light years away from Earth, is a combination of emission, reflection, and dark nebulae and is one of the only night sky objects that contains a yellow nebula. This formation contains sixteen known protostars (or "baby stars") that are not hot enough yet to burn like our sun. Photo taken by Mike Brown of the Chippewa Valley Astronomical Society. Used with permission.

Page 60: Comet C/2023 A3 Tsuchinshan-ATLAS.

Pages 62–63: Comet Neowise (C/2020 F3) over the Chippewa River. Image captured during the COVID-19 shutdown.

Page 64: Comet C/2023 A3 Tsuchinshan-ATLAS. If you look closely, it appears that the comet has two tails: one streaming up and another streaming down. The "counter tail" streaming down is an optical illusion. As a comet travels, it leaves a debris trail in its wake (rather like interstellar breadcrumbs). Before the comet crosses the orbital plane of the Earth, this trail is illuminated by sunlight.

Page 68: Second "diamond ring" moment of totality during the solar eclipse in 2024. Since the surface of the moon has mountains and valleys, the sun peeks through those hills and valleys at different times. It just so happens that the surface formations on the rim of the moon create this beautiful diamond ring appearance.

Page 72: Second "diamond ring" moment of totality during the solar eclipse in 2024.

Page 77: The Rosette Nebula. An emission nebula aptly named for its similarity to a flower, which is more than 5,000 light years away from us. Photo taken by Mike Brown of the Chippewa Valley Astronomical Society. Used with permission.

Pages 78–79: Jellyfish Nebula. Photo taken by Mike Brown of the Chippewa Valley Astronomical Society. Used with permission.

Page 80: NGC 2175 (sometimes called the Monkey Head Nebula). This nebula is more than 6,000 light years away from us. Photo taken by Mike Brown of the Chippewa Valley Astronomical Society. Used with permission.

Page 84: Windmill with Star Trails. The trails (author's first attempt at photographing star trails) represent twenty-three minutes of exposure time. Photo taken from the Geisert family farm.

Pages 86–87: The Milky Way Galaxy — galactic core appears just over the horizon. Photo taken at the Redemptorist Renewal Center in Tucson, Arizona.

Page 90: The Old Amish Mill at Dell's Pond in Augusta, Wisconsin, on a clear, moonlit night.

Pages 92–93: The Milky Way Galaxy. Photo taken at the Redemptorist Renewal Center in Tucson, Arizona, just outside of Our Lady of the Desert Catholic Church.

Page 97: Two open star clusters (ancient galaxies) in relatively close proximity to each other, about 7,500 light years away from Earth. Photo taken by Mike Brown of the Chippewa Valley Astronomical Society. Used with permission.

Page 100: Aurora Borealis (Northern Lights). Photo taken by Old Elk Lake and Muddy Creek Reserve in Wisconsin.

Page 103: Aurora Borealis (Northern Lights). Photo taken by Old Elk Lake and Muddy Creek Reserve in Wisconsin. The "red spear" represents a rare phenomenon called the "forbidden emission line." It occurs when upper atmosphere oxygen is undisturbed for a long period of time and is impacted by stellar winds in a particular way.

Pages 106–107: Panoramic view of the galactic core of the Milky Way Galaxy.

Pages 110–111: Saturn (above) and Jupiter (below) seen after sunset from Shenandoah National Park, Sunday, December 13, 2020, in Luray, Virginia. Science History Images / Alamy Stock Photo

Page 115: The Boogeyman Nebula. Can you see the boogeyman? It's about 500 light years away from us!

Page 116: M78 Nebula. The letter "M" stands for the French astronomer Charles Messier (1730–1817), who had a passion for finding comets. A series of objects he observed were later determined not to be comets, but galaxies and nebulae. M78 is a reflection nebula about 1,600 light years away from us. Photo taken by Mike Brown of the Chippewa Valley Astronomical Society. Used with permission.

Page 120: Good Friday photo of a dead cactus at the Redemptorist Renewal Center in Tucson, Arizona.

Page 123: Kemble's Cascade, sometimes referred to as a waterfall of stars, is roughly 4,000 light years away from us. Photo taken by Mike Brown of the Chippewa Valley Astronomical Society. Used with permission.

Page 128: The Milky Way Galaxy. Photo taken from the Redemptorist Renewal Center in Tucson, Arizona.

Page 131: M13 Star Cluster. Also known as the Hercules Cluster since it is found in the constellation Hercules. It is about 25,000 light years away from Earth. Photo taken by Mike Brown of the Chippewa Valley Astronomical Society. Used with permission.

Page 136: Leo Triplet. A collection of three galaxies in the constellation Leo, about 35 million light years away from Earth. Each of these three galaxies is about the size of our Milky Way Galaxy. Photo taken by Mike Brown of the Chippewa Valley Astronomical Society. Used with permission.

Page 139: Veil Nebula (Eastern). This is half of a massive, circular, supernova-produced nebula that is more than 1,400 light years away from Earth.

Page 140: The Triangulum Galaxy (M33). This is a spiral galaxy found in the constellation Triangulum, about 2.7 million light years away from Earth. It is the third largest galaxy in a local group that includes our Milky Way Galaxy. Photo taken by Mike Brown of the Chippewa Valley Astronomical Society. Used with permission.

Pages 142–143: Galactic core of the Milky Way Galaxy.

About the Author

Fr. James Kurzynski is a priest of the Diocese of La Crosse, Wisconsin, and a hobby astronomer. Originally from the small town of Amherst in rural Central Wisconsin, he completed his undergraduate studies at the University of Wisconsin - Stevens Point, receiving a Bachelor of Arts in Applied Music. After graduating from UW-SP, he worked at the University of Nebraska at Kearney as a Hall Director and pursued a M.S. Ed. in Group Counseling. After a year at UNK, he left his position and graduate studies to discern his priestly vocation at the University of Saint Mary of the Lake/Mundelein Seminary, where he found his calling to be a diocesan priest for the Diocese of La Crosse, Wisconsin.

He earned a bachelor's degree in Sacred Theology, a Master of Divinity, and a License in Sacred Theology. While pursuing these degrees, he also studied Spiritual Theology with the Institute of Priestly Formation at Creighton University and completed the Spiritual Exercises of St. Ignatius of Loyola. He was ordained a priest on June 28, 2003, and has served a variety of assignments ranging from parish and university ministry to teaching Religion, Astronomy, and a number of directed studies courses at Regis High School in Eau Claire, Wisconsin, and Philosophy for Deacon Aspirants.

Father James has been a member of both the Chippewa Valley Astronomical Society and the La Crosse Area Astronomical Society. His first involvement with the Vatican Observatory came when an inquiry led to the development of the first workshop the Vatican Observatory created for nonscientists, now called Astronomy for Catholics in Ministry and Education.